MODELLING THE HUMAN IMPACT ON NATURE

Modelling the Human Impact on Nature

Systems Analysis of Environmental Problems

RICHARD JOHN HUGGETT

OXFORD UNIVERSITY PRESS · OXFORD
1993

Oxford University Press, Walton Street, Oxford OX2 6DP
Oxford New York Toronto
Delhi Bombay Calcutta Madras Karachi
Kuala Lumpur Singapore Hong Kong Tokyo
Nairobi Dar es Salaam Cape Town
Melbourne Auckland Madrid
and associated companies in
Berlin Ibadan

Oxford is a trade mark of Oxford University Press

Published in the United States
by Oxford University Press Inc., New York

British Library Cataloguing in Publication Data
Data available

Library of Congress Cataloging in Publication Data
Huggett, Richard J.
    Modelling the human impact on nature : systems analysis of
environmental problems / Richard John Huggett.
    Includes bibliographical references and index.
    1. Human ecology—Mathematical models. 2. Man—Influence on nature—Mathematical
models. 3. Environmental degradation—Mathematical models. I. Title.
    GF23.M35H85   1993   304.2'01'5118—dc20   93-12093
ISBN 0-19-874170-7
ISBN 0-19-874171-5 (pbk.)

1 3 5 7 9 10 8 6 4 2

Typeset by Best-set Typesetter Ltd., Hong Kong

Printed in Great Britain
on acid-free paper by
Biddles Ltd.
Guildford & Kings Lynn

For Zoë and Ben

and all those of their generation who will experience the changes discussed herein

Preface

It is undeniable that the human species has had, and continues to have, a profound impact on the biosphere. The last three hundred years have seen unprecedented changes in the biosphere, owing to a period of rapid population growth and the rise of an industrial society powered by fossil fuels. Indeed, the changes have been so multifarious and so far-reaching that the biosphere, at the hands of humankind, has been transformed—it has had its fundamental appearance and nature radically changed. That there is a pressing need to understand this transformation is beyond question. Much money, time, and effort is being invested in studies which look at various aspects of the transformation, at the current state of the biosphere, and at changes likely to occur in the near future. The latest exercise in stock-taking is set down in the tome edited by B. L. Turner and others called *The Earth as Transformed by Human Action: Global and Regional Changes in the Biosphere over the Past 300 Years* (1990), a book which reports on early efforts to document and understand the interaction of humankind and the natural world within a long-term, global perspective. It is based on the premiss that the capability now exists to monitor human transformations of the biosphere on the global scale, to estimate with some degree of confidence the transformations over the last several centuries, to identify some of the broad processes which have led to the transformations, and to understand the interactions of these processes on a regional scale.

Invaluable though stock-taking and monitoring may be, deep understanding of global and regional transformations by humans, and the prediction of future transformations, require theoretical models of the processes involved. Modelling is an important tool in investigating changes in environmental systems. Its pivotal role is recognized, for instance, in the International Geosphere–Biosphere Programme, the aim of which is to study the basic processes underlying environmental change at global and regional scales. The present book explores modern approaches to the modelling of regional and global problems associated with the transformation of the biosphere by the human species, highlights the problems and prospects of modelling the human role in regional and global environmental change, and conveys the basic principles of building and using systems models in the context of environmental problems.

I trust that fans of my writings—a very small and select group of perspicacious individuals—will enjoy this, my latest offering. However, they may be disappointed on one count. Whatever the quality of the content, they say, you can always count on Huggett to close with a long bibliography. In this matter, I must confess to failing my faithful audience. Here is my excuse. The book is designed for undergraduates. It tries to encourage them to think big—not of big bibliographies but of big issues of the day, of environmental problems in a global and regional setting. Also, it tries to summon in them the courage to broach that most awesome of subjects—mathematical modelling. I felt it best to limit examples to a few really good ones rather than bombarding trainee modellers with a welter of references which merely cloud the simple picture that I try to paint. In any case, so much teamwork goes on these days that the pages of a richly referenced text would be cluttered by *et al*.s. None the less, I shall not leave my fans crestfallen. They probably expect me to say a few controversial things, so I shall. The impatient can skip now to the last few pages if they desire to confront controversy forthwith. The patient will have to wade through some sixty thousand words before reaching that point. I trust that their patience will have its rewards.

I would conclude by thanking those people who have helped with the production of this book: for taking the book on board, Andrew Schuller and Oxford University Press; for drawing the diagrams, Graham Bowden and Nick Scarle; and, for so much, my wife Shelley.

R. J. H.

Poynton
May 1992

Contents

Part III. Prospects

PART I
Principles

1
Systems and Models

Environmental Systems

The human species, like all species, interacts with its environment. So far as is known, humans, unlike all other species, strive to understand their interaction with the natural world. In endeavouring to make sense of this interaction, we seek patterns and processes in the world around us. To this end, we pick out structures which are stable in form and meaningful in function. Especially useful is the conception of structures as relatively stable forms, storing energy and matter, and existing in, and maintained by, fluxes of energy and matter. Basic structures of this ilk are referred to as systems.

A system is a structure presumed to exist in the real world. It is thought to possess characteristic properties, and to consist of interconnected components. The components are meaningfully arranged, in that they function together as a whole. A forest is a system because it consists of components (trees and other plants, litter, soils, and so on) arranged in a particular way. The arrangement of a forest's components is meaningful because it is explicable in terms of physical processes, and because it acts as a whole. Moreover, forests have characteristic properties which serve to distinguish them from other systems, such as meadow, mire, and moorland. All natural structures with which humans interact may be termed environmental systems.

Models

In trying to single out the components and interrelations of environmental systems, some degree of abstraction or simplification is necessary: the real world is too rich a mix of objects and interactions for all components and relations to be considered. The process by which reality is reduced to manageable proportions is termed model-building. Defined in a general way, a model

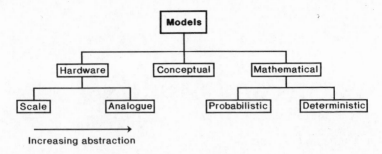

FIG. 1.1. Types of model

is a simplified representation of some aspect of the real world which happens to interest an investigator.

Hardware Models

Models can be built at different levels of abstraction (Fig. 1.1). The simplest level of abstraction involves a change of scale. In this case, the system is represented by a hardware model. There are two chief kinds of hardware model: scale models and analogue models. Scale models, because they closely resemble physically the system they represent, are also termed iconic models. They are miniature, or sometimes gigantic, copies of systems. They differ from the systems they represent only in size. A child's toy train and an architect's model of a building are miniature copies of systems. Three-dimensional structures constructed out of coloured plastic balls and metal or wooden rods are gigantic copies of molecular systems. As well as being useful in teaching, hardware models of molecules have practical value. A crude hardware model gave a clue to the structure of the third stable form of carbon, carbon-60 (also called fullerene), a molecular 'ball' with hexagonal and pentagonal faces arranged exactly as in a football. Static scale models like these have been used to replicate certain aspects of environmental systems. In geomorphology, relief models, fashioned out of a suitable material such as plaster of Paris, have been used to represent topography as a three-dimensional surface. In climatology, the distribution of upper air temperatures has been depicted using models made of glass, and the structure of a cyclone has been described using a model made of wire.

Scale models need not be static: models made using materials identical to those found in nature, but with the dimensions of the system scaled down, can be used to simulate dynamic behaviour. In practice, scale models of this kind imitate a portion of the real world so closely that they are, in effect, a 'controlled' natural system. An example of this is Stanley A. Schumm's (1956) use of the badlands at Perth Amboy, New Jersey, to study the evolution of slopes and drainage basins. The great advantage of this type of scale model, in which the geometry and dynamics of the model and system are virtually identical, is that a high degree of control can be exerted over the simplified experimental conditions.

In other scale models, natural materials are employed but the geometry of the model is dissimilar to the geometry of the system it imitates, the system being scaled down in size. The process of reducing the size of a system creates a number of tricky, but not insuperable, problems associated with scaling. For instance, a model of the Severn Estuary made at a scale of 1:10 000 can fairly easily preserve geometrical and topographical relationships. But, when water is added, an actual depth of water of, say, 7 m is represented in the model by a layer of water less than 0.7 mm deep. In such a thin layer of water, surface tensions will cause enormous problems, and it will be impossible to simulate tidal range and currents. Equally, material scaled down to represent sand in the real system would be so tiny that most of it would float. These problems of scaling can be overcome, to a certain extent at least, and scale models are used to mimic the behaviour of a variety of environmental systems. For example, since the latter half of the nineteenth century, scale models have assisted in the design of civil-engineering projects, and the dynamics of rivers and river systems have been investigated in simple waterproof troughs and more sophisticated flumes. Indeed, it is surprising how many ingenious attempts have been made to replicate the behaviour of environmental systems using scale models. The discussion of this fascinating field is beyond the scope of the present book, but the interested reader should consult Michael Morgan's (1967) paper on the Heath Robinsons of physical geography.

Analogue Models

Analogue models are more abstract refinements of scale models. The most commonly used analogue models are maps and remotely sensed images. On a map, the surface features of a landscape are reduced in scale and represented in symbolic form: roads by lines, relief by contours, and buildings by point symbols, for instance. Remotely sensed images represent, at a reduced scale, certain properties of the Earth's surface. The level of spatial resolution of an image corresponds to the actual size of a pixel (picture element) on the ground. Maps and remotely sensed images are, except where a series of them is available for different times, static analogue models. Dynamic analogue models may also be built. They are hardware models in which the system size is changed, and in which the materials used are analogous to, but not the same as, the natural materials of the system. The analogous materials simulate the dynamics of the real system. So, in a laboratory, the clay, kaolin, can be used in place of ice to model the behaviour of a valley glacier. Under carefully controlled conditions, many features of valley glaciers, including crevasses and step faults, develop in the clay. Difficulties arise in this kind of analogue model, not the least of which is the problem of finding a material which has mechanical properties comparable to the material in the natural system. Electrical analogue models of environmental systems, which use assorted electrical components to represent stores and flows of energy or matter, are not uncommon. Groundwater systems and ecosystems in particular lend themselves to electrical-analogue modelling. In simple ecological applications, energy input is supplied by batteries, energy flow is simulated by electrical currents, and energy dissipation is simulated by amperage and voltage changers.

Conceptual Models

Maps and remotely sensed data are invaluable in monitoring the state of the biosphere and geosphere, and can provide information needed to calibrate and test models of environmental systems. However, to gain a deep understanding of the dynamics of environmental systems, further abstraction is required. This will normally involve the use of a conceptual model.

In brief, a conceptual model expresses ideas about components and processes deemed to be important in a system, and some preliminary thoughts on how the components and processes are connected. In other words, it is a statement about system form and system function. Conceptual models are expressed in several ways: as pictures, as box-and-arrow diagrams, as matrix models, as computer flow charts, and in various symbolic languages (Table 1.1).

Words, Pictures, Boxes, and Arrows

As far as conceptual models are concerned, the old saw is generally true: one picture is worth a thousand words. Verbal descriptions of most environmental systems, where the components and relations are multifarious and complex, become cumbersome and unintelligible. Pictures of environmental systems, in contrast, can convey large amounts of information about composition and spatial structure at a glance. More abstract than pure pictures of systems are box-and-arrow diagrams. The boxes stand for the system components and the arrows depict supposed important links and relations between the components. Because it is the flow of matter and energy through the boxes that is of prime concern, the inner workings of the boxes are not explored in detail. For this reason, box-and-arrow diagrams are sometimes referred to as black-box models. An example is the model of the terrestrial carbon cycle portrayed in Fig. 1.2.

Matrix Representations

Black-box conceptual models can often be converted into input–output models and represented as mathematical matrices. As in an accountant's spreadsheet, the inputs and outputs cascading through the components of an environmental system can be incorporated into a system of rows and columns. The simplest form of matrix is an adjacency matrix. In an adjacency matrix, the system components are the row and column headings. Each element in the matrix represents a flow between the corresponding components. The matrix elements are either 1s or 0s. The 1s in the matrix correspond to an arrow in a box-and arrow diagram, and the 0s correspond to no arrows. As the arrows are directed (they go from one component to another), so are the entries in the matrix: flows are either from rows to columns or from columns to rows. As an example, the flows in the model of the terrestrial carbon cycle shown in Fig. 1.2 are expressed as an adjacency matrix in Table 1.2.

Input–output matrices are created by converting the non-zero

TABLE 1.1. *Conceptual designs of systems*

Model designs	Attributes	Advantages	Disadvantages
Words	Verbal descriptions	Supplement all kinds of conceptualization	Complexity difficult to convey
Pictures	Illustrations using natural elements	Convey spatial characteristics	Lack temporal and mathematical inferences
Black-box diagrams	Components and relations shown as abstract symbols (boxes and arrows)	Emphasize throughputs of matter and energy	Lack mathematical inferences
Input–output matrices	Inputs and outputs of black-box models shown as linear matrix	Concise list of the size of interactions	Lack temporal dynamics and assume linearity
Signed digraphs	Black-box models with logic gates	Qualitative interactions	Lack temporal dynamics and assume linearity
Computer flow charts	Sequential ordering of processes	Components can change in space and time Use logic gates	Interactions not obvious Rudimentary symbolic language
Forrester diagrams	Computer flow charts with feedbacks	Interactions more obvious Rate equations, components, sources, and sinks	
Energy circuits	Complex symbolic language	Computational inferences Thermodynamically constrained Components classed by function	
Unique designs	Combinations and extensions of any of the above		

After Sklar *et al.* (1990: table 1, p. 656).

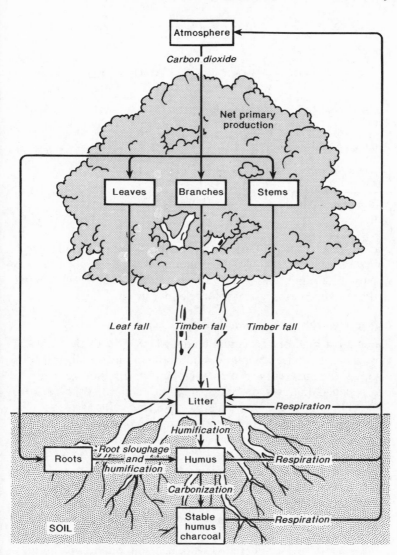

After Goudriaan and Ketner (1984).

FIG. 1.2. The terrestrial cycle of carbon

TABLE 1.2. *Adjacency matrix of terrestrial carbon cycle as depicted in Fig. 1.2*

To		From						
		Leaves x_1	Branches x_2	Stems x_3	Roots x_4	Litter x_5	Humus x_6	Charcoal[a] x_7
Leaves	x_1	0	0	0	0	0	0	0
Branches	x_2	0	0	0	0	0	0	0
Stems	x_3	0	0	0	0	0	0	0
Roots	x_4	0	0	0	0	0	0	0
Litter	x_5	1	1	1	0	0	0	0
Humus	x_6	0	0	0	1	1	0	0
Charcoal	x_7	0	0	0	0	0	0	0

[a] Stable humus charcoal.

entries in adjacency matrices into actual flows. They provide a concise listing of the interactions among system components over a particular time. Table 1.3, for instance, is an input–output matrix of the terrestrial carbon cycle in a tropical forest.

Signed Digraphs and Interaction Matrices

These are a kind of conceptual model which extends the information given in adjacency matrices and box-and-arrow diagrams by 'signing' the interactions. In an adjacency matrix, non-zero entries are assigned minuses or pluses to indicate positive or negative interactions between the system components. This is then called an interaction matrix. In a box-and-arrow diagram, lines ending in a small arrowhead represent positive interactions, and lines ending in a small circle stand for negative interactions; this is called a signed directed-loop diagram, or digraph.

An example of a signed digraph is given in Fig. 1.3, which is a conceptual model of human modifications to the storage of water in lowland soils in eastern North Carolina. Water enters the system as precipitation, is stored in surface depressions and the soil body (as surface-depression storage, soil water, and ground-water), and exits the system as runoff and evapotranspiration. Each link in the system may be allotted a 'sign', plus or minus, depending on whether the link is positive or negative. Precipitation, the input, has a positive influence on both storage and output. Its links with these variables are, accordingly, denoted by lines ending in small arrowheads. Runoff and evapotranspiration,

TABLE 1.3. *Input–output matrix of terrestrial carbon cycle in tropical forests as depicted in Fig. 1.2*

To	From							Input	Output	Row total
	x_1	x_2	x_3	x_4	x_5	x_6	x_7			
x_1	0	0	0	0	0	0	0	8.34	0	8.34
x_2	0	0	0	0	0	0	0	5.56	0	5.56
x_3	0	0	0	0	0	0	0	8.34	0	8.34
x_4	0	0	0	0	0	0	0	5.56	0	5.56
x_5	8.34	5.56	8.34	0	0	0	0	0	0	22.24
x_6	0	0	0	5.56	8.92	0	0	0	0	14.48
x_7	0	0	0	0	0	0.55595	0	0	0	0.55595
Input	0	0	0	0	0	0	0		0	0
Output	8.34	5.56	8.34	5.56	22.23	11.119	0.55594	0	0	61.70494
Column total	16.68	11.12	16.68	11.12	31.15	11.67495	0.55594	27.8	0	126.78089
Cycling efficiency	0.5	0.5	0.5	0.5	0.286	0.04761	0			

Mean path length:
126.78089/27.8 = 4.56

Note: The stores are denoted by the xs. x_1 is leaves, x_2 branches, x_3 stems, x_4 roots, x_5 litter, x_6 humus, and x_7 stable humus charcoal. The flows of carbon are expressed as Gt C/yr (see Appendix).

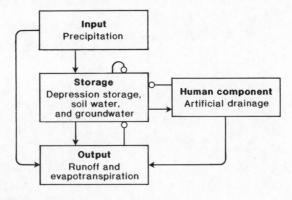

After Phillips (1991).

FIG. 1.3. A signed digraph

TABLE 1.4. *The interaction matrix of the soil water system in eastern North Carolina as depicted in Fig. 1.3*

		Water input x_1	Water storage x_2	Water output x_3	Artificial drainage x_4
Water input	x_1	0	a_{12}	a_{13}	0
Water storage	x_2	0	$-a_{22}$	a_{23}	a_{24}
Water output	x_3	0	$-a_{32}$	0	0
Artificial drainage	x_4	0	$-a_{42}$	a_{43}	0

After Phillips (1991: table 4, p. 325).

the output, has a negative influence on storage, being derived from stored water released between precipitation events. Its links with storage are thus denoted by a line terminating in a small circle. Water storage is self-limiting: there is an upper limit to the amount of water soil can store. This property is indicated by a closed loop. To an extent, the store regulates the output: the more water stored, the greater the outflow (especially via groundwater flow); the less water stored, the smaller the output, since water is held at higher tensions: hence the positive link from storage to output. The human component, which may seek to maintain water storage at the level most favourable to crop growth, is connected to the rest of the system in the following manner: storage has a positive influence on humans, who strive to manipulate the system, using canals, ditches, and so forth, to increase withdrawals; in turn, the withdrawals have a positive link with output, because they increase it.

The signed digraph shown in Fig. 1.3 is readily converted to an interaction matrix (Table 1.4). The connections are expressed by the letter a, with subscripts signifying the variables involved. So, a positive connection between precipitation, variable 1, and soil water storage, variable 2, is denoted by a_{12}. All other connections are labelled using the same logic.

Flow Charts

Computer programmes are commonly designed using flow charts. Given a specific problem, flow charts are used to work out a logical sequence of computations for finding a solution. It is possible to apply the same method in the solution of problems concerned with environmental systems. The sequence of events in a flow chart will then represent an assumed ordering of environmental processes. Once the flow chart is translated into a programming language, the model can be run and, if all goes well, a solution to the problem suggested. A drawback with using flow charts as conceptual models is that the type of interaction occurring within a compartment of the flow chart is not evident. Normally, the name of a subroutine, but little else more informative, is mentioned. Fig. 1.4 shows a flow chart for a simple spatial model used in Chapter 3. The model is designed to predict the changing storage of nitrogen within a landscape. Although the chart gives an idea of the overall structure of the computational procedure, it is uninformative on several counts. For example, it fails to indicate the precise nature of the equations used to calculate change in nitrogen storage. It does not make obvious, therefore, the fact that the rate constants for nitrogen transfer between grid-cells are determined by topographical slope gradients.

Analogue computer diagrams are another kind of computer flow chart model. Analogue symbols are used to represent storages and flows of energy or matter as a system of electrical voltages and currents. Popular in the early 1960s, before digital computers became widely available, analogue computers are little used today in the study of environmental systems.

Symbolic Languages

Some writers have created their own sophisticated versions of box-and-arrow diagrams in which the roles that components play

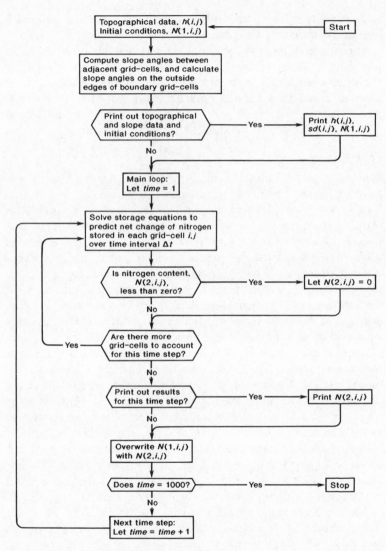

FIG. 1.4. A computer flow chart

in a system are indicated pictorially. Standard 'roles' are represented by a set of canonical structures, that is, basic functional units whose operation need not be resolved at a lower level of resolution. Like fashion designers, the creators of symbolic systems of canonical structures do not lack imagination: so many different schemes have been offered that the chances ever of agreeing on a standard form are slim. However, two symbolic languages have caught on, and are commonly employed. The first is the creation of Jay W. Forrester. It is basically a computer simulation language written, initially at least, to tackle industrial and urban problems. Later, it was extended to the so-called world simulation described in *World Dynamics* (1971). The chief canonical structures in Forrester's systems dynamics language are state variables, shown by valves; auxiliary variables that influence the rate of processes, drawn as circles; flows of people, goods, money, energy, and so forth, represented by solid arrows; causal relationships, denoted by broken arrows; and sources and sinks of energy and mass, portrayed as clouds.

Another symbolic language which enjoys widespread currency was devised by Howard T. Odum (1971; 1983). Odum's energy-circuit language, called energese, comprises several modules, each a canonical structure, joined by lines representing flows of energy. In isolation, the modules in this language look like the doodlings of an eccentric electrical engineer (Fig. 1.5). Energese is, however, a succinct way of capturing in pictorial form an enormous amount of information about the components and relations within systems.

In energese, solid lines show flows. Circles stand for potential energy sources, such as sun and wind (Fig. 1.5a). The symbol which looks like a house with a rounded base stands for passive stores of energy (1.5b). Arrows going to ground are heat sinks, and depict that portion of energy which is dissipated as heat while work is being done (1.5c). Combined with arrows going to ground, the passive energy-store symbol represents the storage of new potential energy against some storage force, a process requiring work to be done and hence energy dissipation (1.5d). The short bullet-shaped symbol stands for the reception of pure wave energy (such as sound, light, water waves, and wind) and its interaction with a combined cycling receptor and self-maintaining module (1.5e). In this module, energy interacts with a material cycling round the system producing an energy-activated state,

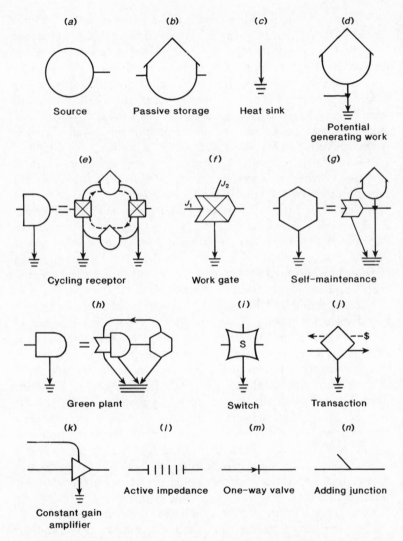

Source: Odum (1971). (Copyright © 1971 John Wiley & Sons, Inc. Reprinted by permission.)
FIG. 1.5. Modules of Howard T. Odum's electrical circuit language called energese

which then returns to its deactivated state passing energy on to the next step in a chain of processes. The kinetics of this module was first discovered in the reaction of an enzyme with its substrate, and is named the Michaelis–Menton reaction, after its discoverers. The pointed block (a sort of stubby arrow) is a work gate, and represents the work done by a system component in procuring energy from sources outside the system; it acts as a kind of control valve (1.5f). The hexagon represents a self-maintaining subsystem (1.5g). It is a combination of two modules—a work gate and a potential energy store—which act in concert to ensure that the energy stored is fed back to control the work done by the whole unit. An example is a trophic level of an ecosystem. The long bullet-shaped symbol is a combination of a self-maintaining module and a cycling receptor (5h). Energy captured by the cycling receptor is fed to the self-maintaining unit, which in turn keeps the cycling machinery working, and returns necessary materials to it. A green plant is an example. The small square with concave edges represents flows which have 'on' and 'off' states, and which control other flows by switching actions (1.5i). The small lozenge-shaped symbol is used to denote transactions in systems involving flows of money (1.5j). Four other symbols are used (1.5k, l, m, and n) to represent constant gain amplifiers, active impedance (which allow a backforce to develop in the system), one-way valves, and additive junctions. All the afore-mentioned units may be assembled to represent actual systems. By way of example, look at the stores and flows of materials in a bottomland hardwood forest expressed in energese (Fig. 1.6); a dynamic model of this system will be discussed in Chapter 7.

Yet another symbolic language, originating in the hydrological literature, was adopted by Richard J. Chorley and Barbara A. Kennedy in their influential *Physical Geography: A Systems Approach* (1971) to depict physical process-response systems. Arthur N. Strahler and A. H. Strahler (1973, 1974), father and son, modified Odum's energese, so devising their own method of portraying the energetics of environmental systems. To meet the needs of the wide range of systems encountered in physical geography, Arthur N. Strahler (1980) made further revisions to the language. Other schemes have been suggested, but we shall not describe them. The point to make is that there are several commonly used symbolical languages for presenting conceptual

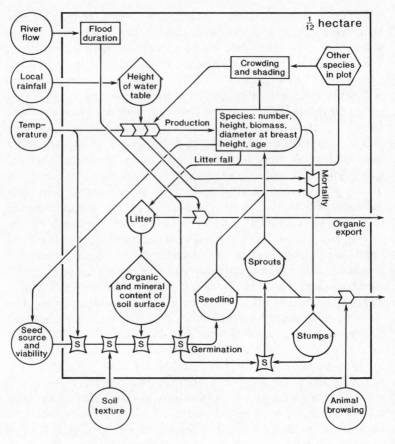

After Pearlstine *et al.* (1985).

FIG. 1.6. Stores and flows in a bottomland hardwood forest expressed in energese

models of systems. Each has advantages and disadvantages. Any attempt to come up with a definitive set of symbols is probably futile. It is far better to spend time thinking about the components and relations in the system being depicted than it is to agonize over the method of depiction.

Conceptual Models as Hypotheses

It is crucially important to be aware that any system can be conceived of in many ways: there are potentially an astronomically huge number of conceptual models of any system. This is because no model can ever be fully correct and achieve identity with the system it represents. The corollary of this fact is that the nature of a system can never be truly or thoroughly known, but will always remain, to some extent, a matter of conjecture. For this reason, a system is itself a kind of conceptual model, the existence of which in reality often rests upon nothing more than shared intuition. A system is a concept which, like beauty, lies in the eyes of the beholder; it is an idea, a hypothesis about how some portion of reality is assembled and how it works (Huggett, 1985: 8). This point is absolutely fundamental but commonly neglected. The risk is that shared intuition may lead to an aspect of the nature or dynamics of a system being accepted without question, the necessarily hypothetical nature of the system being overlooked. Take an example. It has been dogmatically accepted for decades that, whereas materials circulate around ecosystems, energy passes through as a one-way flow. The danger of this dogma is that the hypothetical nature of the view that energy transfer is a one-way flow may be forgotten. A few years ago, Bernard C. Patten (1985) convincingly demonstrated that, although it differs from matter in its dissipation, energy *does* circulate in ecosystems: the dogma has been overturned and the textbooks need rewriting!

Conceptual models help to clarify loose thoughts about how a system is composed and how it operates. Therefore, they are often used as a foundation for the construction of mathematical models, the chief subject of this book. And yet the process by which conceptual models are devised is seldom given the deliberation it warrants. The dynamics predicted by a model of a system depend very much on the system components selected and the relationships assumed to exist between them. Early astronomers grouped stars into constellations which, we now believe, have no meaning. Today stars are grouped into galaxies and galaxy clusters, a conceptual arrangement which seems to make far more sense. This is an extreme example, but it serves to stress that the building of conceptual models is not something to be done lightly: it is the most important step in the entire process of mathematical modelling. As Fred H. Sklar and his colleagues put it (1990: 625), the conceptualization of a system is the backbone of the entire process of mathematical model-building.

Mathematical Models

Mathematical model-building involves translating the ideas encapsulated in a conceptual model into the formal, symbolic logic of mathematics. The language of mathematics offers a powerful tool of investigation limited only by the creativity of the human mind. Of all modes of argument, mathematics is the most rigorous. It furnishes a means of describing a system in a symbolism which is universally understood. Mathematical models seem capable of giving the deepest insight into how environmental systems work, of providing the best means of predicting change in environmental systems, and of affording the most trustworthy guide as to how best to manage or control environmental systems. This is not to say that mathematics can replace the intuition and inspired guesses of environmental scientists. Rather, it offers a standardized way of formalizing thoughts and ideas, and a potent means of analysing problems. Of course, mathematical models merely provide a guide to the credible environmental repercussions of specific human actions. They are uninformative on matters political, philosophical, and moral. None the less, mathematical models allow experiments to be run on environmental systems, and generate realistic output which can be used as the basis for rational and informed environmental management policies. That, at least, is the hope. In practice, the irrational side of human nature seems often to come to the fore, as in the reluctance of the United States government to accept the reality of global warming as induced by 'greenhouse' gas emissions, despite the repeated warnings uttered by the climate-modellers.

The act of quantification, of translating ideas and observations into symbols and numbers, is in itself nothing: it must be validated by explanation and prediction. The art and science of using mathematics to study environmental systems is to discover expressions with explanatory and predictive powers. Mathematical models are pregnant with power. It is this power which sets mathematical models apart from conceptual models. An unquantified conceptual model is not susceptible of formal proof; it is simply a body of ideas. A mathematical model, on the other hand, may be tested by matching predictions against the yardstick of observation. By a continual process of mathematical model-building, model-testing, and model redesign, the understanding of the form and function of environmental systems, and of the role of human activity in them, should improve.

Stochastic and Statistical Models

Three chief classes of mathematical model are used to study environmental systems: stochastic models, statistical models, and deterministic models. The first two classes are probabilistic models. Stochastic models have a random component built into them which describes a system, or some facet of it, on the basis of probability. Statistical models, like stochastic models, have random components. In statistical models, the random components represent unpredictable fluctuations in laboratory or field data which may arise from measurement error, equation error, or the inherent variability of the objects being measured. A body of inferential statistical theory exists which determines the manner in which the data should be collected and how relationships between the data should be managed. Statistical models are, in a sense, second best to deductive models: they can be applied only under strictly controlled conditions, suffer from a number of deficiencies, and are perhaps most profitably employed only when the 'laws' determining system form and process are poorly understood.

The present book will not address probabilistic models in much detail. It will be assumed that the reader is familiar with inferential statistical techniques, such as correlation and regression, and these will not be discussed. Stochastic models are commonly used in conjunction with deterministic models to simulate the behaviour of some environmental systems, such as stands of trees in a forest whose growth has a strong probabilistic element. Where appropriate, an explanation of stochastic models will be given.

Deterministic Models

Deterministic models are conceptual models expressed mathematically and containing no random components. They can be derived from physical and chemical principles without recourse to experiment. It is sound practice, therefore, to test the validity of a deterministic model by comparing its predictions with independent observations made in the field or laboratory. Deterministic models come in a variety of forms, the most useful of which in studying the human impact on environmental systems are dynamical system models. Evolved from open-system theory, dynamical system models involve a set of system components acting as a whole. They are concerned with change and susceptibility to change in systems, and are used to predict the transfer and transformation of energy and matter in environmental systems. In addition, they provide a theoretical base for the new generation of mathematical models dealing with dissipative structures, multiple equilibria, bifurcations, and catastrophes. These fascinating models generate probabilistic-type elements from deterministic relations.

And so, without further ado, we shall pass on to the nitty-gritty of the mathematical modelling process. Chapters 2 and 3 will lay down the basics of the modelling procedure, considering system state, systems relations, and systems dynamics. The remaining chapters will elucidate the practice of mathematical modelling by examining cases where mathematical models have proved especially enlightening in the study of environmental systems. We shall consider energy balances, biogeochemical cycles, water cycles, and life cycles. Finally, we shall look into the prospects of modelling the human impact on nature.

2

System States and Relations

System Variables

State Variables

The condition of environmental systems is described by state variables. As their name implies, state variables are measures of system components whose values vary with time. Two types of variable are used to characterize a system: variables defining constitutional properties and variables defining configurational properties. The constitution of environmental systems is measured by such things as mass, concentration, acidity, and vegetation cover; the configuration of environmental systems is measured by properties pertaining to size and shape, such as slope angle, area, and tree diameter.

The simplest environmental system is defined by just one state variable. Take the example of the carbon cycle in the terrestrial biosphere, as shown in Fig. 1.2. Single out one component of the system—the litter lying on the soil surface. This litter system may be defined by one state variable—the amount of carbon in the litter store at a given time. Denote this state variable as

$$x_{litter,t} = \text{carbon stored in litter at time } t$$

Now, it is possible to study the carbon balance of the litter system in isolation; but, to gain a fuller appreciation of the cycling of carbon in the biosphere, it would be better to expand the model to include more system components (stores of carbon). Assuming for the moment that we are interested in just one other store—humus—then we need to define a second state variable to describe the amount of carbon stored in humus. Express this second variable as

$$x_{humus,t} = \text{carbon stored in humus at time } t$$

The system now comprises two state variables, x_{litter} and x_{humus}. For simplicity, the state variables can be put in matrix form and expressed as **x**. In our example, **x** is a vector containing two elements, one for each state variable. Written in full, **x** looks like this:

$$\mathbf{x} = \begin{bmatrix} x_{litter} \\ x_{humus} \end{bmatrix}$$

To add even more realism to the model, we may enlarge the system yet again to include another store of carbon—stable humus charcoal. Denote this third system component as

$x_{charcoal,t}$ = carbon stored as stable humus charcoal at time t

The system now comprises three state variables, x_{litter}, x_{humus}, and $x_{charcoal}$. Expressed in matrix form, the three-component system is written as a vector, **x**, containing three elements, one for each state variable:

$$\mathbf{x} = \begin{bmatrix} x_{litter} \\ x_{humus} \\ x_{charcoal} \end{bmatrix}$$

In a more general case, we may define system state variables as $x_1, x_2, \ldots x_n$. In matrix form, this reduces to **x**, where **x** is a state vector which, written in full, looks like this:

$$\mathbf{x} = \begin{bmatrix} x_1 \\ x_2 \\ \vdots \\ x_n \end{bmatrix}$$

Driving Variables

Systems are bounded. Within a system's boundary lie the system components; outside its boundary lies the environment, or surroundings, of the system. State variables outside the system are exogenous or external variables; those inside the system are endogenous or internal variables. In our model of the terrestrial carbon cycle, we may place bounds on the system in many ways. For example, we might choose to locate the upper bound at the interfaces between the atmosphere and vegetation and between the atmosphere and the land surface. The lower bound we might set as the bottom of the soil profile. Carbon crossing the upper boundary of the system, as carbon dioxide from the air, would thus be an exogenous variable. And carbon stored in the system—in litter, in humus, and as stable humus charcoal—would then be described by endogenous variables. On the other hand, we could limit the system of interest to the humus store. In this case, the carbon stored in litter and as stable humus charcoal would be exogenous variables, and the carbon stored in the humus store would be an endogenous variable.

Systems which lack exogenous variables are unforced systems; those with exogenous variables are forced systems. Environmental systems are normally defined as forced systems, for without energy and material supplied to them by exogenous variables, they would run down. Because of this, exogenous variables are referred to as driving variables or forcing variables. In the model of the carbon cycle, the driving variable is the net primary production of vegetation. The primary production creates a store of carbon which keeps the system running. However, the system could be studied as an unforced system, for example when looking at the depletion of the carbon stores after burning and clearing, or the decay of a single tree which has fallen to the forest floor.

A distinction is often drawn between systems whose boundaries are open to the transference of matter and energy—open systems—and systems whose boundaries are open only to the passage of energy—closed systems. Environmental systems are normally studied as open systems. Moreover, because environmental systems dissipate energy in order to maintain themselves, they can be categorized as dissipative systems.

State Change

The state of a system may be supposed to change either continuously, or else over discrete slices of time. In a model, if a continuous time formulation is adopted, then system state is traced through infinitesimally small steps of time; in this case, we write dt to stand for an infinitesimally small increment of time. If, on the other hand, a discrete time formulation be stipulated, then system state may be tracked in jumps between finite steps of time; in this case, we write Δt to stand for a finite period of time. The difference between the two formulations should become clear when we examine a concrete case. Take our model of carbon flow and storage in the terrestrial biosphere. We have specified that the amount of carbon stored in litter at time t is:

$$x_{litter,t}$$

After an infinitesimally small lapse of time, the amount of carbon stored in the litter may be denoted as

$$x_{litter,t+dt}$$

and, after the passing of a finite period of time, it may be denoted
as

$$x_{litter,t+\Delta t}$$

The rate of change in carbon storage over the time interval is, in
both cases, derived by subtracting the amount of carbon stored at
the start of the time interval from the amount of carbon stored at
the end of the time interval, and then dividing by the duration of
the time interval (Fig. 2.1). So, we may write:

$$\text{Rate of change of carbon storage} = \frac{(x_{litter,t+dt} - x_{litter,t})}{dt}$$

$$\text{Rate of change of carbon storage} = \frac{(x_{litter,t+\Delta t} - x_{litter,t})}{\Delta t}$$

Letting

$$x_{litter,t+dt} - x_{litter,t} = dx$$

and

$$x_{litter,t+\Delta t} - x_{litter,t} = \Delta x$$

then the time rates of change may be expressed as follows:

$$\frac{\text{Rate of change of}}{\text{carbon storage}} = \frac{dx}{dt} \quad \text{(continuous formulation)}$$

$$\frac{\text{Rate of change of}}{\text{carbon storage}} = \frac{\Delta x}{\Delta t} \quad \text{(discrete formulation)}$$

Both continuous and discrete time formulations are widely used in
models of environmental systems.

State Space

If a system has more than one state variable, then its condition at
any time can be plotted within what is known as the state space of
the system. The state space is created by using the values of the
state variables as co-ordinates. Each state variable is a co-ordinate,
and all co-ordinates stand at right angles to each other. In the case
of just two state variables, there are two co-ordinates, one for
each state variable, and the state space is a two-dimensional state
plane. Any point within this state plane uniquely defines the
condition of a system at a particular time. We could define a two-
dimensional state plane for the carbon-cycle model using the

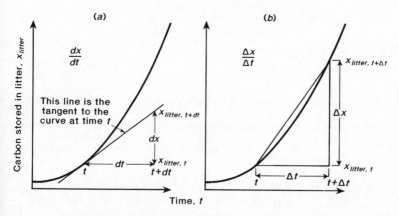

FIG. 2.1. Formulations of time rates of change: (a) continuous change, dx/dt; (b) discrete change, $\Delta x/\Delta t$.

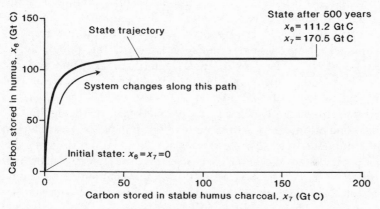

FIG. 2.2. A state plane defined by two state variables in the terrestrial carbon model—humus, x_6, and stable humus charcoal, x_7

stores of carbon in humus and stable humus charcoal as co-ordinates. Any point in the state plane, then, uniquely defines the system state in terms of the amount of carbon in each of the stores. Changes in the state of a system are traced within the state space by a line (trajectory) produced by a series of points. An example is given in Fig. 2.2, which shows the trajectory traced in the two-dimensional state space of the system. The system starts

TABLE 2.1. *Combinations of time and state space formulations and the kinds of equation associated with them*

Time	State space	
	Continuous	Discrete
Continuous variable	Partial differential equations	Ordinary differential equations
Discrete variable	Partial difference equations	Ordinary difference equations

with empty stores and shifts along the trajectory shown. In the general case, with n state variables, the state space will have n dimensions and will be defined by n Cartesian co-ordinates.

State space, like time, can be treated as continuous or discrete. There are four possible combinations of time and state-space formulations (Table 2.1). In a continuous time, continuous state-space formulation, partial differential equations are used to describe the rate of change of system variables. An example is a model of an animal population wherein the population is expressed as a function of time, t, and age, a. Time and age are both independent variables, so that there are two rates of change—time rate and age rate. Because of this, we write the partial differential coefficients $\delta x/\delta t$ and $\delta x/\delta a$, which signify that the population varies with more than one independent variable. In a continuous-time, discrete state-space formulation, ordinary differential equations are used to describe the rate of change of system variables. In the case of the age distribution of an animal population, there would be an ordinary differential equation describing the dynamics of each discrete age-class. With a discrete time, continuous state-space formulation, partial difference equations are employed. With a discrete time and discrete state-space formulation, ordinary difference equations are used. The derivation and use of these equations will become clear later in the book.

Aggregated and Disaggregated Models

Aggregated Models
In our model of carbon storage in a litter system, the system was treated as a single unit and described by just one state variable.

Moreover, the spatial distribution of carbon storage in litter across a forest floor was not a feature of the model. Models of this sort, which focus on one, or several non-interacting, state variables in a particular area, are called aggregated models. The litter system is one example. Another is a model which considers the number of tree species in a region through time. In aggregated models, any of the four permutations of continuous and discrete time and state-space formats may be used. Although aggregated models of environmental systems have their uses, more complex disaggregated models are usually preferred, since they present a more realistic picture of a system.

Distributional Models

It is usually desirable to disaggregate an environmental system into a set of interacting components, or into a set of interacting spatial elements, or into both. Models which represent systems as a set of interacting components, but which do not take explicit account of the spatial variations in state variables, may be called distributional models. They are so called because they take on board the distribution of one or several variables among system components in a particular region. A distributional model of an animal population, for instance, would define the system components as classes pertaining to age and sex; and it would define state variables as the number of individuals in each age and sex class. Similarly, a distributional model of a forest might define the system components as the different vegetation communities in a region, and the state variables as the number of individual tree species. The model would thus look at the 'distribution' of individual tree species among different communities in an area. In like manner, our model of the terrestrial carbon cycle looks at the 'distribution' of carbon among a set of interacting components—litter, humus, stable humus charcoal—in a particular area.

Distributional models may engage any of the four combinations of continuous and discrete representations of time and state space set down in Table 2.1. In distributional models which take time as a continuous variable, and regard state space as continuous, then one or several partial differential equations are employed to describe the system of interest. Such equations are used in models which investigate biological populations, and have potential for exploring the age–size distribution of patches of different land uses and vegetation in a landscape. Where time is treated as a continuum, and state space is taken as discrete, then a set of ordinary differential equations is used to describe the system of interest. Such equations are used to model change in species composition in plots of vegetation. The original models of this ilk were known by the acronyms JABOWA and FORET; they, and their offspring, will be discussed in Chapter 7. Briefly, they consist of a set of differential equations describing the growth of individual trees by species (the discrete states) in small plots of land.

In distributional models which take time as a discrete variable, and see state space as continuous, then one or several partial difference equations are used to describe the system of interest. The application of these equations to environmental systems is rare. It would include models of biological populations in which age and size are considered conjointly in distinct generations. Where time is taken as a discrete variable, and state space is also treated as discrete, then ordinary difference equations are used, usually in matrix form for cases with several state variables. All distributional models using difference-equation, discrete state-space formulations may be expressed, in their simplest form and in matrix notation, as:

$$\mathbf{x}_{t+1} = \mathbf{A}\mathbf{x}_t$$

where $\mathbf{x}_t$ is a column vector whose elements, x_1 to x_m, are state variables, and $\mathbf{A}$ is an $m \times m$ matrix whose elements, a_{ij}, incorporate inputs, outputs, and transfers between states occurring during the interval between time t and time $t + 1$. $\mathbf{A}$ thus determines the transition from one state to another and is called a transition matrix. Three widely used forms of difference-equation, distributional models are Markov-chain models, semi-Markov models, and Leslie matrix models.

Markov-chain models are stochastic, since the transition between discrete states i and j is expressed as a transition probability, p_{ij}. Their use is to some extent restricted by the assumptions that change is determined only by current states and transition probabilities, which means that the history of the system is not taken into account; and that the transition probabilities stay constant over time. None the less, Markov-chain models have been used with success in the modelling of change in animal populations, in the composition of vegetation during succession, and in land-use change. Semi-Markov models allow for a state sojourn time by letting the length of time that a system component has been in discrete state i influence the probability of transition to discrete state j. They are little used in the study of environmental systems, although they have potential for modelling some aspects of landscape change. Leslie matrix models were originally developed to project change in the age and sex structure of biological populations. They use a deterministic transition matrix to define shifts between system states. Models for projecting change in human populations are elaborations of the original Leslie matrix model. They are highly sophisticated, and include thousands of endogenous and exogenous variables.

Spatial Models

Models which represent systems as a set of interacting components, and which take explicit account of the spatial variations in state variables, may be called spatial models. They are so called because they take on board the location and spatial configuration of one or several variables among system components. Spatial models use the location and configuration of system components in projecting change, and predict the values of state variables at various points within a system. In general, the space occupied by environmental systems—their spatial domains—may be studied in one, two, or three dimensions. Many models constructed over the last decade consider the change in state variables across the two-dimensional space of the land surface, and within the three-dimensional volume of the atmosphere and the oceans.

In all spatial models, it is necessary to divide the spatial domain of the system of interest into subregions. The size and shape of the subregions are defined arbitrarily. They are geared to the problem being studied, the availability of data, and the level of spatial detail required in different parts of the spatial domain. In environmental applications, the simplest kind of spatial cell is a cuboid or block. Blocks can be built up to fill the space under investigation. To study processes in a soil profile they may be stacked; to model flow in a river they may be placed end to end in a line; to study landscape processes in two dimensions they may be placed side by side; and to study three-dimensional processes they may be placed side by side as well as stacked. Other shapes are used: lakes are often represented by slices of water placed one upon another. However, a common practice is to employ either a two-dimensional grid (raster) of equal-area, square, or rectangular grid-cells, also known as pixels (picture elements), or a set of polygons, which may or may not be equal in area. Following William L. Baker (1989: 121), we shall call the full collection of grid-cells or polygons 'mosaics', and the component units 'cells'. With a continuous state space, each cell has a single value for each state variable: with a discrete state space, each cell contains a single state for each state variable. It is also possible to adopt a vector-based format in which the locations of system components (for instance, trees) are specified by the x and y co-ordinates of points, lines, or polygons outlining the component—for example, the grid reference of a point representing a tree.

Two sorts of spatial model are distinguished: component models, in which change in individual system components is modelled; and mosaic models, in which change in a mosaic of individual sub-regions is modelled. Component models are, to date, exclusively biological. They consider the response of individual organisms to the spatial location, character, and density of organisms living nearby. Commonly, neighbourhood effects are quantified as indices of competition. The models may allow for the dispersal of organisms and lateral growth. They have been built to study neighbourhood effects in trees, annual plants, shrubs, and sessile marine organisms. Mosaic models are applied to the full range of environmental systems and will be examined in a little detail.

Mosaic models are of two kinds: aggregate mosaic models and distributional mosaic models. In an aggregate mosaic model, the state variable assumes just one value—in the case of a continuous state space—or one state—in the case of a discrete state space—in each grid-cell. It is common for these models to present state variables as a two-state 'chequerboard'. Individual grid-cells might be designated occupied–unoccupied, land–water, or forest–clear-cut. Aggregate mosaic models are in the early stages of development. They have been profitably applied in the simulation of land-use changes, mainly those associated with forest succession and disturbance, especially by clear-cutting. A model which looked at the spatial variation of one or several state variables within a spatial domain would also be an aggregate mosaic model. An example is a model of tree-species diversity in a region represented as a set of grid-cells. In distributional mosaic models, each grid-cell contains information about the state of several system components. In the case of a population, information on the number of individuals in each age and sex class is predicted. And in the case of a forest, each grid-cell comprising the spatial domain of the forest houses information on the system components (the different communities in the forest) and the state variables (the number of individual tree species in each of the communities).

Mosaic models may employ continuous or discrete mathematics. In the continuous state-space formulation, the spatial domain occupied by a system is regarded as a continuum in all directions. It is normally defined in Cartesian co-ordinates—two horizontal, x and y (map co-ordinates), and one vertical, z. Occasionally, polar co-ordinates, r and Θ are used. Whatever the co-ordinate system opted for, state variables are assumed to vary continuously throughout the spatial domain of the system. In the case of carbon stored in the soil, carbon content at a given point could be denoted by $x_{soil}(x, y, t)$. General circulation models of the atmosphere and oceans (which will be dealt with in detail in Chapter 4) are, arguably, the most complex and sophisticated mosaic models. They predict the values of some two dozen state variables from a large set of differential equations for a grid-cell network covering the globe. Each cell may be as small as $2° \times 2°$ (latitude $\times$ longitude) in size. There is also a battery of distributional mosaic models which present state space as a set of discrete spatial units. Multi-regional population models keep account of thousands of endogenous and exogenous state variables in tens of geographical areas. Similar models have been built to predict spatial interaction between population, residential location, work-place location, the development of infrastructure and transport systems, job location, location of services, and economic development. Although these models have not yet been married to environmental systems, they have potential for simulating landscape changes by human action in rural settings. The multi-regional population models have their counterparts in biology, where they are used to simulate animal and plant populations, albeit at a small scale.

Hierarchies of Systems

Levels of Interest

On the basis of their boundaries, systems are normally defined in terms of three levels: the level of interest, or the system chosen for

study; the level within, or the system components; and the level
without, or the environment. Take a tropical rain forest as the
system of interest. Then components of the tropical rain forest—
animals, plants, litter, and soil—would be the level within; and
the environment of the tropical rain forest—the rest of the biosphere—would be the level without. By defining a system, its
components, and its environment in this way we are imposing a
hierarchical structure on nature. This is acceptable since most
environmental systems appear to be organized on a hierarchical
basis. Indeed, it is fashionable to view the natural world as a
nested series of systems within systems, each system being at the
same time a thing in its own right and a part of a bigger, more
inclusive thing.

It is generally true that systems occupying each echelon of a
hierarchy display a degree of autonomy over their component
parts and over their environment. This autonomy is in part
achieved by the systems at a given echelon functioning at different
scales of time and space from systems on the higher and lower
echelons. In a tropical rain forest, the relatively fast and frequent
day-to-day contacts between individual animals and plants pass
virtually unnoticed in the annual turnover of matter and energy in
the entire forest; instead, they appear to be in a more or less
steady state. At the other extreme, the global biogeochemical
overturnings of the biosphere are relatively slow compared to the
changes in the rain forest, where they appear as roughly constant
influences—they are driving variables which seem to be regular
and well-behaved. Another example, shown in Fig. 2.3, shows the
echelons in the hierarchy of systems in the region of the Mississippi
Delta. The delta region of the Mississippi River can be considered
as a system with inputs and outputs of matter and energy. Various
hydrological subsystems can be recognized within the deltaic area,
each of which imports and exports materials and energy, and each
of which comprises several interacting components—swamps,
bayous, brackish marsh, fresh aquatic beds, and so on. In turn,
each of these components consists of a set of smaller components
(such as surface water, sediments, and plants), each of which is a
system in its own right.

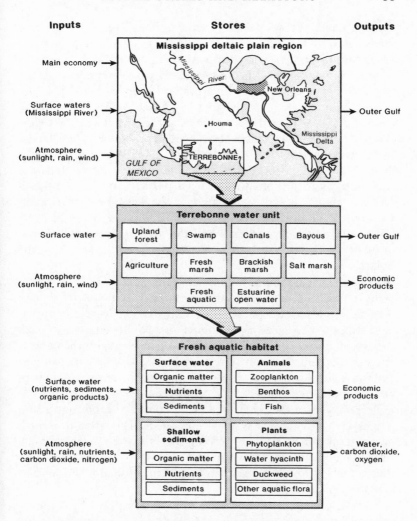

FIG. 2.3. The hierarchy of ecosystems in the Mississippi Delta region

Holons and Environs

Although systems at all levels of a hierarchy behave with a high degree of autonomy, there will invariably be some connections between the system of interest, its parts, and its environment: nothing exists in true isolation. The connections are bipartite. On the one hand, the system of interest is linked to its component subsystems; on the other hand, it is linked to a larger supersystem, or environment, of which the system is a component part. A system residing in any echelon of a hierarchy of systems thus has two faces: the face turned towards the lower level, towards the system components or subsystems, is that of an autonomous whole; the face turned up, towards the environment or super-system, is that of an independent part. To describe these Janus-faced structures, Arthur Koestler (1967; 1978) coined the term 'holon', after the Greek word *holos*, meaning a whole, plus the suffix *on*, as in proton, suggesting a particle; and he entitled a series of nested holons a 'holarchy'. The behaviour of a holon will reflect an attempt to reconcile the forces by which the holon asserts its independence and the forces which tend to sub-ordinate the dynamics of the holon to a larger-scale system in the holarchy.

Adopting the notion of holons, Bernard C. Patten (1978; 1982) defined 'environs' as basic units of ecology. It is important to note that, in doing so, he recognized two distinct environments associ-ated with the two faces of all holons: one is afferent, and stops at the system component—this is the input environment; the other is efferent, and starts at the system component—this is the output environment. An environ consists either of a system component and its input environment (a 'creaon'), or else of a system com-ponent and its output environment (a 'genon'). A creaon–genon pair is then a holon, or system component. The environ, though not a term widely used by ecologists, is the key element in a formal mathematical theory of abiotic and biotic systems. This theory has led to the proposing of a system of dual inheritance to explain evolution.

Several holarchies of environmental systems have been identi-fied: they include the atmospheric holarchy, the tectonic holarchy, the geomorphological holarchy, the pedological holarchy, the genealogical holarchy, and the ecological holarchy. There is no agreed system of naming the holons of which these holarchies are built. Here are two examples which have been proposed: the ecological holarchy runs from individual organisms, through local communities, communities, and biomes, to zonobiomes; and the pedological holarchy runs from soil horizons, through soil pedons, and soil catenae, to soil landscapes (see Huggett, 1991: 9–12).

System Relations

Cascades

Environmental systems may be characterized by inputs, outputs, and storages. Fig. 1.2, for instance, depicts the carbon cycle in a terrestrial ecosystem as seven interacting components—plants (divided into leaves, branches, stems, and roots), litter lying on the ground, humus, and stable humus charcoal. The seven components are linked by a continuous circulation of carbon. Carbon enters the system as the gas carbon dioxide through the plant leaves. It is incorporated into the plants as primary production, and then moves through the system along the following route: from plant leaves to litter by the process of leaf fall; from plant branches and stems to litter by the process of timber fall; from plant roots to humus by the process of root sloughage (the rotting, or humification, of roots); from litter to humus by the process of humification; and from humus to stable humus charcoal by the process of carbonization. It leaves the system as gaseous carbon dioxide produced by the respiration of plants (in leaves, branches, stems, and roots), and by the respiration of organisms in litter, humus, and stable humus charcoal. Notice that, in passing through the system, carbon is stored in the system components and travels through them to emerge as output, and that the output of one component forms the input of another. Thus, carbon entering plant leaves is stored in plant-leaf tissue and lost from the plants in leaf fall. The leaf fall then creates an input to the litter component, which in turn stores carbon and loses carbon by the processes of humification and respiration. There is thus a cascade of carbon as it wends its way through the system and its components.

Most environmental systems involve cascades of matter. Examples are the water cascade—the input, storage, and output of water (and ice) in all systems of the hydrosphere, including lakes, rivers, and drainage basins; and the weathering and debris cascade—the input, storage, and output of sediments and solutes in a landscape.

Rules of Storage

The passage of energy and matter through environmental systems is not a haphazard process: there are rules or laws which determine the rate, and sometimes the direction, of transfer between system components, such as the transfer of carbon from plants to litter, of energy from plants to herbivores, and the number of births in a population. These rules apply to outputs which pass into the environment (the space lying outside the spatial domain of the system), but not normally to inputs from the environment: the loss of energy in respiration is partly under the control of the system, but the amount of sunlight entering the system is determined by factors outside the system's influence. The transfer and storage of mass and energy in environmental systems are subject to basic laws, the two most important of which are the laws of conservation and the laws of flow (also called process laws and transport laws).

The laws of conservation may be expressed as balance equations. Put simply, balance equations are a statement of the fact that what goes into a system must be stored, come out, or be transformed into something else: matter, energy, and momentum cannot appear or disappear in an unaccountable manner. For energy transactions, the energy balance is defined by the first law of thermodynamics, or principle of energy conservation. This states that energy may be transformed from one form to another, but it is neither created nor destroyed. In practice, this means that the change in the amount of energy stored in a system during a time interval must equal inputs of energy less outputs of energy over that period. Thus we may write a general energy balance or energy storage equation as

> change in energy storage
> = (energy inputs − energy outputs) time interval

For convenience, we may denote energy storage by E (with the change in energy storage being written dE), the energy inputs by E_{in}, the energy outputs by E_{out}, and the time interval by dt. This enables us to write the energy balance equation as

$$dE = (E_{in} - E_{out})dt$$

Dividing both sides of the equation by the time interval, dt, yields another commonly used form of the energy balance equation:

$$\frac{dE}{dt} = E_{in} - E_{out}$$

where dE/dt is the time rate of change of energy storage. If the equation be applied to a spatial system, then spatial terms, usually expressed with reference to Cartesian co-ordinates x, y, and z, must be added. The principle of energy conservation is important in the study of all environmental systems, and it has proved especially rewarding in the case of ecosystems.

For mass transactions, the law of mass conservation, sometimes referred to as the continuity condition, applies. It enables us to write a mass storage, or continuity-of-mass, equation:

change in mass storage
= (mass inputs − mass outputs) time interval

For convenience, we may denote mass storage by M (with the change in mass storage being written dM), the mass inputs by M_{in}, the mass outputs by M_{out}, and the time interval by dt. This enables us to write the mass storage equation as

$$dM = (M_{in} - M_{out})dt$$

Dividing both sides of the equation by the time interval, dt, yields another commonly used form of the mass storage equation:

$$\frac{dM}{dt} = M_{in} - M_{out}$$

where dM/dt is the time rate of change of mass storage.

For animal and plant populations, the law of mass conservation applies (in the sense that all individuals must be accounted for) and we may write, as it were, a population storage equation:

change in population size
= (population inputs − population outputs) time interval

Denoting population size by N (with the change in population size being written dN), the population inputs by N_{in}, the population outputs by N_{out}, and the time interval by dt, we may write the population storage equation as

$$dN = (N_{in} - N_{out})dt$$

Dividing both sides of the equation by the time interval, dt, yields another commonly used form of the population storage equation:

$$\frac{dN}{dt} = N_{in} - N_{out}$$

where dN/dt is the time rate of change of population size.

Rules of Flow

The second group of laws—the flow, process, or transport laws—serves to define the inputs and outputs which appear in the storage equations. Take the output of carbon from litter occurring by respiration. This process may be defined by a transport law. We might assume that the amount of carbon lost in respiration over a time interval is proportional, by some constant factor, to the amount of carbon stored in the litter. The relation would be expressed as

> carbon output in respiration
> = constant × amount of carbon stored in litter

Call the constant k. This constant has important applications in many branches of science. It goes by two names: rate constant and transfer coefficient. Rate constants have the dimensions of reciprocal time, T^{-1} (for instance, per year). They signify the proportion of material in a store which is replaced during a unit interval of time. We may write the respiratory loss of carbon from the litter as

$$\text{output} = kx_{litter}$$

More generally, output may be defined by a response or output function, which we shall call g. The output function depends on the system state and the inputs. So we have

$$\text{output} = g(\text{state, inputs})$$

In the litter system, the system state is the amount of carbon in the litter, x_{litter}. Now, the litter may be thought of as a stock of carbon atoms which, during a specified interval of time, are topped up by leaf fall and timber fall, and depleted by humification and respiration. For the general case, the incoming and outgoing fluxes of carbon may be represented by the letter F. Denoting inputs as F_{in} and outputs as F_{out}, we may write an output function in the form

$$F_{out} = g(x_{litter}, F_{in})$$

The exact form of the output function, g, has to be determined, and will be discussed in the next chapter.

Now, in the face of changing outputs and inputs, the state of the system—the amount of carbon stored in litter—may vary with time. As a general rule, given the state of a system at a particular time, the system state after an interval of time has elapsed will be determined by:

1. the state of the system at the commencement of the time interval;

2. a function which defines the inputs and outputs during the time interval: f(outputs, inputs); and
3. the duration of the time interval.

Using the following symbolism for the litter system:

$$x_{litter,t} = \text{state at start of time interval, time } t$$
$$x_{litter,t+1} = \text{state at end of time interval, time } t + 1$$
$$\Delta t = (t + 1) - t = \text{the duration of the time interval}$$

we may write

$$x_{litter,t+1} = x_{litter,t} + f(\text{outputs, inputs})\Delta t$$

The outputs in the function f(outputs, inputs) depend, as determined by the output function, g, on system state and inputs; so we may express the equation as

$$x_{litter,t+1} = x_{litter,t} + f(\text{state, inputs})\Delta t$$

The function f(state, inputs) is called a state transition function, because it determines how the state changes from one time to another.

We have now at our disposal the basis of a model of the litter system. This leads us to the next step in the modelling process and the important issue of the dynamics of systems, the subject of the next chapter.

3

System Dynamics

We concluded the previous chapter by defining state transition functions and output functions. A system for which both a state transition function and an output function exist is termed a dynamical system. Most environmental systems are dynamical. To see how measures of system state and rules of flow can be shaped into a working model, and to explain how such a model can be used to explore the dynamics of a system, we shall start by taking the simple case of a system defined by one state variable, and then erect successively more complex models, ending with the general case of n state variables.

Simple Systems

The dynamics of a system are revealed by solving the storage equations simultaneously. To solve the storage equations, three things must be specified: the starting state, system parameters, and the values of driving variables. If all these conditions be defined, then the system is fully calibrated and the solution to the equations will predict the values of the state variables as the system changes. In the simplest case of a system described by just one state variable, it is usually possible to solve the storage equation by analytical means. In more complex cases, where there are many state variables and non-linear relationships, a numerical solution is normally necessitated.

A Litter System

To clarify the above points, take that portion of the model of carbon storage and flow through the terrestrial ecosystem as outlined in Fig. 1.2 which deals with the amount of carbon stored in litter lying on the land surface. Isolating the litter store, we define a litter system (Fig. 3.1). This system has one component,

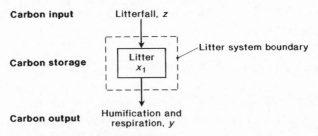

FIG. 3.1. A litter system defined by a state variable describing the amount of carbon stored in litter, x_1, carbon inputs from litterfall, z, and carbon outputs in humification and respiration, y

litter, described by one state variable, the amount of carbon stored in the litter. The system gains carbon through litterfall. Incoming carbon originates outside the system boundaries, so it is a driving variable and may be designated z. Outgoing carbon goes two ways: to the air, as carbon dioxide produced in respiration; and, by the process of humification, to a humus store, regarded as lying outside the system as we have defined it. These outgoing flows may be lumped together and designated y. By drawing up the inputs and outputs of carbon, we may write a system storage (or system state) equation:

$$\frac{dx}{dt} = z - y$$

The term $z - y$ is the state transition function of the system. It is simply a list of all input and output terms. We saw in the previous chapter that the outputs may be defined, in a general way, by an output function, g, which depends on system state and the inputs:

$$\text{output} = g(\text{state, inputs})$$

As outputs are state-determined, the state transition function depends only on system state and inputs and may be written:

$$f(\text{state, inputs}) = z - y$$

The inputs, z, need to be specified when calibrating the model. They would depend on the type of ecosystem being considered. A realistic figure for a temperate forest would be $240\,\text{g C/m}^2/\text{yr}$. The outputs, y, must be defined by an output function (process law). It is reasonable to assume that the carbon released by litter decay, y, is proportional by a factor, k, to the amount of carbon held in store, x:

$$y = kx$$

The storage equation then reads:

$$\frac{dx}{dt} = z \qquad - kx$$

$$\text{inputs} \qquad \text{outputs (determined by}$$
$$\text{the state of the system)}$$

The parameter k is a rate constant or transfer coefficient. It has the dimensions of reciprocal time, T^{-1}. It can be measured in field experiments or, in the example, it could be calculated by dividing input by the carbon storage in the litter at steady state. With an input of $240\,g\,C/m^2/yr$, and a steady-state storage of $600\,g\,C/m^2$, k is $240/600 = 0.4$ per year. The reciprocal of the rate constant is the turnover time. In the example it is $1/0.4 = 2.5$ years. The turnover time represents the amount of time needed to replace all the carbon held in store under steady-state conditions. With 40 per cent of the carbon being replaced every year ($k = 0.4$), it takes 2.5 years to change all the carbon present. The turnover time has three aliases: the time constant, the residence time, and 'life-span'. All four terms have the same physical significance, expressing the ratio of throughput to storage. They thus indicate how much of the input is stored and how much emerges as output during an interval of time.

An Analytical Solution

Now, the carbon-storage equation, being a first-order ordinary differential equation, has an analytical solution. This means that it can be integrated to yield an algebraic function expressing the state variable, x, as a function of the initial state of the system, x_0, the system parameters, z and k, and time, t. We shall not derive the solution, but here it is:

$$x = z/k - (z/k - x_0)e^{-kt}$$

The resulting curve, for the case where the litter store of carbon starts out empty, is plotted in Fig. 3.2. It shows that the amount of carbon stored in the litter changes asymptotically to a certain limit where inputs are balanced by outputs. The limit is the steady or stationary state and is defined by z/k, which in the example is $240/0.4 = 600\,g\,C/m^2$. Simple but effective equations of this kind

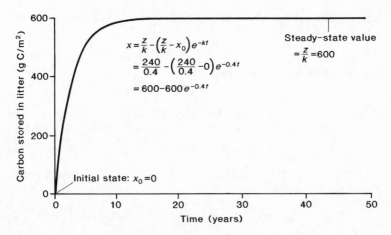

Note: Parameters: carbon input, $z = 240\,\mathrm{g\,C/m^2/yr}$; rate constant, $k = 0.4/\mathrm{yr}$. Notice that the steady-state storage, when carbon input balances carbon output, is given by $z/k = 240/0.4 = 600\,\mathrm{g\,C/m^2}$.

FIG. 3.2. The dynamics of the litter system starting from zero storage (which might represent the condition after a forest fire)

were being used to study changes in soil fertility half a century ago by Hans Jenny (e.g. 1941: 256).

A Numerical Solution

Most models of environmental systems, especially distributional and mosaic models, will be too complex to possess analytical solutions. The alternative is to solve the system equations using a numerical method. We shall see how this is done by solving the carbon-storage equation using a numerical technique known as the Euler method. The first stage is to write the carbon-storage equation as a finite difference approximation, so called because infinitesimally small increments are approximated by finite steps:

$$\frac{x_{t+1} - x_t}{\Delta t} = z - kx$$

Rearranging, we get

$$x_{t+1} = x_t + (z - kx)\Delta t$$

The time interval, Δt, is equal to $(t + 1) - t$.

For this equation to be solved, it must first be calibrated.

Adding the parameter values which were used in the analytical solution, we have:

$$x_{t+1} = x_t + (240 - 0.4x)\Delta t$$

Starting at time zero, we write

$$x_{t=1} = x_{t=0} + (240 - 0.4x)\Delta t$$

In the example used earlier, the state (the amount of carbon in the litter store) at time zero was $0\,g\,C/m^2$, so we have

$$x_{t=1} = 0 + (240 - 0.4x)\Delta t$$

Setting the time interval, Δt, as one year, we can compute the state after one time step:

$$x_{t=1} = 0 + \{240 - (0.4 \times 0)\} \times 1.0 = 240\,g\,C/m^2$$

This value can then be substituted in the equation

$$x_{t=2} = x_{t=1} + (240 - 0.4x)\Delta t$$

to find the state after two time steps. Doing the computations, we get

$$x_{t=2} = 240 + \{240 - (0.4 \times 240)\} \times 1.0 = 384\,g\,C/m^2$$

By continued number-crunching, we may calculate the state after any number of time steps (see Table 3.1 and Box 1).

It is important to realize that the Euler method provides an approximation to the exact solution of differential equations and involves errors. Two errors exist: truncation errors and rounding errors. Rounding errors arise from the fact that a computer stores quantities to a certain number of decimal places; because of this, at each time step a tiny rounding error occurs which, over many steps, may grow to be a large error. Truncation errors stem from the fact that Euler's equation approximates a continuous curve as a series of discrete, straight-line sections. The truncation error, ε, is

$$\varepsilon = \frac{1}{2}(\Delta t)^2 \frac{d^2x}{dt^2} + \text{higher-order terms}$$

The smaller the time step, Δt, the smaller the truncation error and the greater the stability of the numerical solution. Halving the time interval Δt reduces truncation error by a factor of four. On

TABLE 3.1. *The effect of the time interval, Δt, on the solution obtained by the Euler method. Storage values are g C/m^2*

Time (yrs)	Analytical solution	Numerical solution (Euler method) with time interval, Δt, set at				
		0.1 yr	1 yr	3 yr	5 yr	7 yr
0	0	0	0	0	0	0
1	197.81[a]	201.10	240.00			
2	330.40	334.80	384.00			
3	419.28	423.69	470.40	720.00		
4	478.86	482.78	522.24			
5	518.80	522.07	553.34		1200.00	
6	545.57	548.19	572.01	576.00		
7	563.51	565.55	583.20			1 680.00
8	575.54	577.10	589.92			
9	583.61	584.77	593.95	604.80		
10	589.01	589.90	596.37		0	
11	592.63	593.27	597.82			
12	595.06	595.53	598.69	599.04		
13	596.69	597.03	599.22			
14	597.78	598.02	599.53			−1 344.00
15	598.51	598.69	599.72	600.19	1200.00	
16	599.00	599.13	599.83			
17	599.33	599.42	599.90			
18	599.55	599.61	599.94	599.96		
19	599.70	599.74	599.96			
20	599.80	599.83	599.98		0	
21	599.87	599.89	599.99	600.01		4 099.20
22	599.91	599.92	599.99			
23	599.94	599.95	600.00			
24	599.96	599.97	600.00	600.00		
25	599.97	599.98	600.00		1200.00	
26	599.98	599.99	600.00			
27	599.99	599.99	600.00	600.00		
28	599.99	599.99	600.00			−5 698.56
29	599.99	600.00	600.00			
30	600.00	600.00	600.00	600.00	0	
31	600.00	600.00	600.00			
32	600.00	600.00	600.00			
33	600.00	600.00	600.00	600.00		
34	600.00	600.00	600.00			
35	600.00	600.00	600.00		1200.00	11 937.41
36	600.00	600.00	600.00	600.00		
37	600.00	600.00	600.00			
38	600.00	600.00	600.00			
39	600.00	600.00	600.00	600.00		
40	600.00	600.00	600.00		0	
41	600.00	600.00	600.00			
42	600.00	600.00	600.00	600.00		−19 807.30
43	600.00	600.00	600.00			
44	600.00	600.00	600.00			

TABLE 3.1. (*cont.*)

Time (yrs)	Analytical solution	Numerical solution (Euler method) with time interval, Δt, set at				
		0.1 yr	1 yr	3 yr	5 yr	7 yr
45	600.00	600.00	600.00	600.00	1200.00	
46	600.00	600.00	600.00			
47	600.00	600.00	600.00			
48	600.00	600.00	600.00	600.00		
49	600.00	600.00	600.00			37 333.20
50	600.00	600.00	600.00		0	

[a] Figures rounded to 2 decimal places.

BOX 1. *A computer model to simulate a simple litter system*

This box contains a computer program which will run the model of the simple litter system described in the text. The program, and the others given later in the chapter, are written in Microsoft MS-DOS QBasic and designed to run on IBM-PC compatible machines. Providing that they are keyed in correctly, they should run on any PC, though some minor modifications may be necessary, especially with the PRINT statements. As the programs stand, the output is sent to a monitor screen. By adding a few appropriate additional lines (the details of which should be explained in the manual to your PC), the output could be sent to a printer. In this case, LPRINT statements in the first and second programs would need to print the output lines under one another, rather than in the same position, at each time step.

The litter system program will ask you to specify the initial storage of carbon x_0 (g C/m^2), the carbon input through litterfall z (g C/m^2/yr), the rate constant for litter loss y (/yr), the time interval for integration Δt (yr), and the total number of time steps to be simulated. To check that the program is working correctly, run the program and input the figures given in the text for the case of a temperate forest when requested to do so: initial carbon storage 0; carbon input in litterfall 240; rate constant for litter loss 0.4; time interval 0.1; total number of time steps 600. Running with these values should generate the same figures as in Table 3.1 for $\Delta t = 0.1$ yr.

Once you have combed out all the bugs from your program, you can explore the effects that changing the inputs and outputs has on steady-state store sizes of carbon. For example, you might run the program to establish the steady-state storage of carbon in the litter of (1) a tropical forest and (2) a boreal forest. In a tropical forest, a carbon input in litterfall of 500 g C/m^2/yr and a rate constant for litter loss of 2.0 per year are fairly typical figures. The steady-state value in this simplest of models is readily found without recourse to numerical simulation: it is $500/2.0 = 250$ g C/m^2. Does the model confirm this value? Running the model for a boreal forest, where the carbon input in litterfall is about $50 \, g \, C/m^2/yr$ and the rate constant for litter loss is about 0.05 per year, should yield a steady-state value of $50/0.05 = 1000 \, g \, C/m^2$. Does the model confirm this value? Use the model to discover how long it takes the litter system to reach a steady state in each of the three forest types. Try to interpret the differences that occur.

It is highly instructive to experiment with varying time intervals of integration. Try running the temperate forest model with the following time intervals: $\Delta t = 0.001, 0.01, 0.1, 0.5, 1.0, 3.0, 5.0$, and 10.0. Note that, when $1/y$ is greater than Δt, the program will warn you that the solution will be unstable. To see what happens under these circumstances, you must simply opt to 'press on regardless' when prompted to do so.

```
REM
REM Program to explore the dynamics of a litter system
REM
REM x is carbon stored in litter (grammes per square metre)
REM
COLOR 11, 1, 1
DIM x(1001)
20 REM
LET rerun = 0
CLS
PRINT "Simulation run for litter system"
PRINT
INPUT "Initial litter storage (grammes per square metre) = "; h(1)
INPUT "Litterfall rate (grammes per square metre per year) = "; z
INPUT "Rate constant for litter loss (per year) = "; y
10 INPUT "Time interval, dt (years) = "; dt
IF 1 / y > dt THEN GOTO 30
BEEP
PRINT "WARNING: dt too large for a stable solution"
PRINT "You may either press on regardless or else try again using dt<="; 1 / y
INPUT "Carry on (enter 1) or try again (enter 2)"; retry$
IF retry$ = "2" THEN GOTO 10
INPUT "dt = "; dt
30 REM
INPUT "How many time steps (maximum 1000) "; tt
INPUT "After how may time steps do you wish the program to pause"; pwait
INPUT "Do you wish to run with these parameters (y/n)"; go$
IF go$ = "n" THEN STOP
CLS
REM
REM Main loop to solve litter storage equation using Euler method
REM
FOR t = 1 TO tt
LET x(t + 1) = x(t) + (z - y * x(t)) * dt
NEXT t
REM
REM Display results
REM
PRINT "Litter system dynamics "
PRINT
PRINT "Initial storage"; x(1); "grammes of carbon per square metre"
PRINT "Litterfall"; z; "grammes of carbon per square metre per year"
PRINT "Rate constant for litter loss"; y; "per year"
PRINT "Time interval"; dt; "years"
PRINT
PRINT "     Time      Time     Litter storage"
PRINT "     step      (yr)     (g C/m2/yr)"
PRINT
VIEW PRINT 11 TO 12
LET tc = 0
FOR t = 1 TO tt
LET tc = tc + 1
PRINT USING "##########.##"; t; (t - 1) * dt; x(t)
IF tc = pwait THEN GOSUB Halt
```

```
VIEW PRINT 11 TO 12
IF t = tt THEN GOSUB Finish
IF rerun = 1 THEN GOTO 20
NEXT t
Halt:
VIEW PRINT 14 TO 15
PRINT
PRINT "Press any key to continue"
DO
LOOP WHILE INKEY$ = ""
PRINT
LET tc = 0
RETURN
Finish:
VIEW PRINT 14 TO 18
PRINT
PRINT "Simulation run over. Press any key to continue"
DO
LOOP WHILE INKEY$ = ""
PRINT
INPUT "Have another go (y/n)"; run$
IF run$ = "n" THEN STOP
LET rerun = 1
VIEW PRINT 1 TO 18
RETURN
```

the other hand, the shorter the time step the longer the computing time, and the greater the possibility of rounding errors.

More sophisticated methods of solving differential equations by numerical means are available. Basically, these higher-order methods compute the first derivatives at different points of time within the integration time step, and then calculate the higher derivatives according to the way in which the first derivatives change. Examples are the trapezoidal method and the Runge–Kutta method. Higher-order methods give good results if the system equations are well-behaved and the driving variables are given as continuous functions. Where these conditions are not met, and sometimes even when they are, higher-order methods have a propensity to generate spurious results. Where the rate constants in the differential equations vary widely over different time-scales, it is advisable to employ what are called stiff equations. Choosing a suitable method is no mean task. However, it is probably worth trying the underrated Euler method in the first instance. The Euler method has the advantage of being elegantly simple. This simplicity means that all the steps in the calculation can be readily checked out to see what is happening. Using this method, the prudent modeller will integrate his or her system equations across a range of integration intervals, Δt, to assess the stability of the solution. The perils of not doing so are grave. In extreme cases, where the time interval is rather large, unstable oscillations may arise, causing the computer programme to crash. The real danger, though, is a case where unstable oscillations occur but are not severe enough to halt the programme: the unwary might erroneously assume that the oscillations reflect the behaviour of the system itself! This effect is shown in Table 3.1, which presents numerical solutions of the litter system obtained using the Euler method with different time intervals, including long ones which generate unstable solutions.

The Modelling Procedure

In summary, the procedure for building a dynamic mathematical model of an environmental system runs like this (Thomas and Huggett, 1980: 64):

1. State problem or hypothesis.
2. Make definitions and assumptions:
   (*a*) Define system of interest, including boundaries, components, inputs, and outputs;
   (*b*) Draw up storage equations, one for each component;
   (*c*) Define inputs and outputs in storage equations using transport laws.
3. Calibrate the set of equations.
4. Run the model and test the results.

This is simply a statement of the basic steps commonly taken when constructing mathematical models. It should not be taken as a list of hard-and-fast rules for all modelling activity. Modelling is both an art and a science. The artistic part comes into play in the early stages when the system of interest is being conceptualized. It involves finding the components and relations which seem best to represent the system being modelled. Additionally, it may entail taking cognizance of economic factors in the modelling process itself: many models cost a not insignificant amount of money to build, to run, and to calibrate using empirical data. Where money is a constraint, these costs must be set against the benefits likely to accrue from the predictions coming from the model.

Complex Systems

Usually, a system of interest will consist of several components, and not just one as in the case of the litter system. A model of a multi-component system will comprise a set of state equations, one equation for each component. Because the output of one component may become the input of another, the equations relate to processes which proceed hand in hand; they are therefore termed simultaneous equations. If the equations deal with changes over infinitesimally short time steps, they are called simultaneous differential equations; if they deal with change over discrete steps of time, they are called simultaneous difference equations.

Carbon in the Terrestrial Biosphere

As an example of a complex system, we shall develop a model of the storage and flux of carbon in the ecosystems of the terrestrial biosphere, as presented in conceptual form in Fig. 1.2. In the model, a terrestrial ecosystem is represented as seven interacting components—plants (divided into leaves, branches, stems, and roots), litter lying on the ground, humus, and stable humus charcoal. The amount of carbon stored in each of these components is a state variable. It is convenient to use symbols to stand for the state variables. We shall define the state variables as follows: x_1 is the amount of carbon stored in leaves, x_2 is the amount stored in branches, x_3 is the amount stored in stems, x_4 is the amount stored in roots, x_5 is the amount stored in litter, x_6 is the amount stored in humus, and x_7 is the amount stored in stable humus charcoal.

The seven state variables are linked by a continuous circulation of carbon. Carbon enters the system as the gas carbon dioxide through the plant leaves, and is incorporated into the plants (leaves, branches, stems, and roots) as primary production. Some of the primary production is burnt up in respiration; the remainder constitutes the net primary production of the ecosystem. The system is driven by net primary production, which we may label as z. In the model, net primary production is partitioned among the four components of plants: leaves, branches, stems, and roots. The partitioning is accomplished by means of coefficients, $p_{i,v}$, where the subscript v ($v = 1$ to 6) identifies the ecosystem type (Table 3.2), and the subscript i ($i = 1$ to 4)

	Tropical forest[a] (v = 1)	Temperate forest[b] (v = 2)	Grassland (v = 3)	Agricultural area (v = 4)	Human area (v = 5)	Tundra and semi-desert (v = 6)
Driving variable, z_v (Gt C/yr):						
Net primary production	27.8	8.7	10.7	7.5	0.2	2.1
Partition coefficients, $p_{i,v}$ (fraction):						
Leaves ($i = 1$)	0.3	0.3	0.6	0.8	0.3	0.5
Branches ($i = 2$)	0.2	0.2	0	0	0.2	0.1
Stems ($i = 3$)	0.3	0.3	0	0	0.3	0.1
Roots ($i = 4$)	0.2	0.2	0.4	0.2	0.2	0.3
Transfer coefficients (rate constants), k_{ij} (/yr):						
Leaves to litter	1.0	0.5	1.0	1.0	1.0	1.0
Branches to litter	0.1	0.1	0.1	0.1	0.1	0.1
Stems to litter	0.033	0.0166	0.02	0.02	0.02	0.02
Roots to humus	0.1	0.1	1.0	1.0	0.1	0.5
Litter to humus	1.0	0.5	0.5	1.0	0.5	0.5
Humus to charcoal	0.1	0.02	0.025	0.04	0.02	0.02
Charcoal to environment	0.002	0.002	0.002	0.002	0.002	0.002
Transfer factors (fraction):						
Humification factor, b_v	0.4	0.6	0.6	0.2	0.5	0.6
Carbonization factor for humus decomposition, c_v	0.05	0.05	0.05	0.05	0.05	0.05
Areas (10^{12} m²)	36.1	17.0	18.8	17.4	2.0	29.7

[a] Comprises tropical forest, forest plantation, shrub-dominated savannahs, and chaparral.
[b] Comprises temperate forests, boreal forests, and woodlands.

Source: Data from Goudriaan and Ketner (1984).

identifies the plant component (1 for leaves, 2 for branches, 3 for stems, and 4 for branches). The four partition coefficients must sum to 1.0.

Carbon moves through the system. To identify the fluxes, we make use of the fact that there will be a source (donor) store from which emanates the carbon, and a terminal (receptor) store by which the carbon is received. For instance, carbon passes from plant leaves, state variable x_1, to litter, state variable x_5, by the process of leaf fall. This flux within the system may be denoted by F_{15}. Carbon also passes from plant branches, state variable x_2, and stems, state variable x_3, to litter, state variable x_5, by the process of timber fall. These fluxes may be denoted F_{25} and F_{35} respectively. By the same token, carbon movement from plant roots to humus by the process of root sloughage (the rotting, or humification, of roots) may be denoted as F_{45}; from litter to humus by the process of humification as F_{56}; and from humus to stable humus charcoal by the process of carbonization as F_{67}.

Carbon leaves the system as gaseous carbon dioxide produced by the respiration of plants (in leaves, branches, stems, and roots), and by the respiration of organisms in litter, humus, and stable humus charcoal. These fluxes pass from the system to the environment. In the litter system described at the start of the chapter, we denoted outputs by y. We could write the output from state variable x_1 to the environment as y_1, from state variable x_2 to the environment as y_2, and so on. Alternatively, the environment may be thought of as state variable x_0. So, carbon lost by respiration in the litter store may be signified as F_{50}. All other fluxes exiting the system could be labelled in like manner: F_{10}, F_{20}, F_{30}, F_{40}, F_{60}, F_{70}.

The system is powered by carbon entering the system from its environment. We identified net primary production as the driving variable and denoted it as z. It could also be denoted as four separate fluxes F_{01}, F_{02}, F_{03}, and F_{04}, since it is a flux from the environment of the system, state variable x_0, to plants, comprising four separate state variables, x_1 to x_4. Both systems of notation are encountered in the ecological literature.

The full system of state variables and carbon fluxes is presented in Fig. 3.3. To model the flux of carbon through the system, we need to draw up a storage equation for each state variable. These equations will define the time rate of change of the state variables,

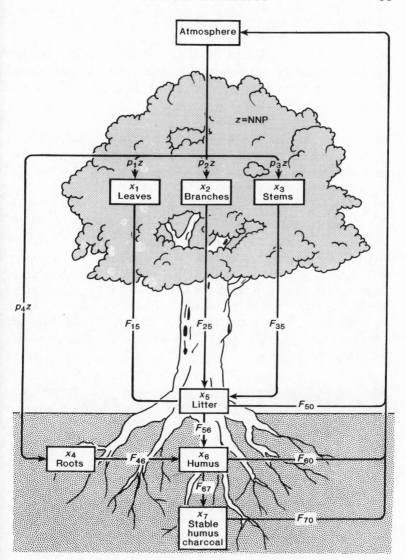

FIG. 3.3. State variables and fluxes in the terrestrial carbon system

dx_i/dt, as the difference between the incoming and outgoing fluxes of carbon. For the first four state variables—the carbon stored in various parts of plants—the incoming carbon is the driving variable net primary production. For a given ecosystem, z is partitioned among the leaves, branches, stems, and roots. The inputs for leaves may thus be written

$$\text{inputs} = p_{1,v}z_v$$

where $p_{1,v}$ is the partition coefficient for ecosystem v, and z_v is net primary production for the ecosystem. Leaves lose carbon to the litter store by leaf fall, the flux for which is F_{15}. The storage equation for the leaves is thus

$$\frac{dx_1}{dt} = p_{1,v}z_v - F_{15}$$

The output of carbon from leaves occurs as leaf fall. This process may be defined by a transport law. We may assume, for example, that the amount of carbon lost in leaf fall over a time interval is proportional, by a factor k, to the amount of carbon stored in the leaves. The factor k is a rate constant or transfer coefficient with the units of reciprocal time. Denoting the transfer coefficient of flow from state variable i to state variable j as k_{ij}, we may write the output for leaves as

$$\text{output} = k_{15}x_1$$

Similar storage equations may be written for all state variables (cf. Fig. 3.4). The equation for litter, x_5, is more complex because it has input terms coming from leaves, branches, and stems:

$$\text{inputs} = k_{15}x_1 \quad\;\; + k_{25}x_2 \quad\;\; + k_{35}x_3$$

| input from leaves | input from branches | input from stems |

Carbon is lost from the litter store by humification. It is reasonable to define this process by a linear decay equation in which the amount of carbon lost during a time interval is directly proportional, by a transfer coefficient k, to the amount of carbon in the litter store:

$$\text{outputs} = k_{56}x_5$$

Putting inputs and outputs together, we have

$$\frac{dx_5}{dt} = k_{15}x_1 + k_{25}x_2 + k_{35}x_3 - k_{56}x_5$$

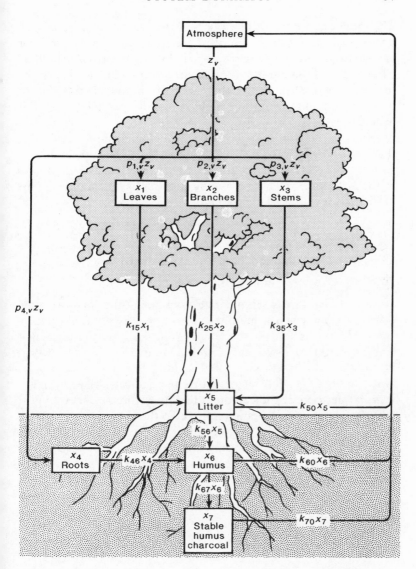

FIG. 3.4. The terrestrial carbon system with fluxes defined by transport laws

The inputs and outputs of carbon in the humus store must take account of the fact that not all the carbon released by the litter enters the humus pool: some of it is lost to the environment as carbon dioxide in respiration. We may accommodate this in the model in two ways: either the losses of carbon dioxide due to humification and respiration could be listed separately; or else, if it be not necessary to keep specific account of respiratory losses, a humification factor may be used. The humification factor, h, defines the fraction of outgoing carbon from the root and litter stores which enters the humus store (the remaining fraction goes to the atmosphere). Using a humification factor, the inputs for the humus store would be defined as

$$\text{inputs} = h_v(k_{56}x_5 + k_{46}x_4)$$

When a specific account of respiratory losses is required, separate terms for respiration and humification are listed:

$$\text{inputs} = k_{56}x_5 + k_{46}x_4$$

However, the values of the rate constants—the ks—are now different from when a humification factor was used. To understand why this is so, take the rate constant for litter to humus in a tropical forest as listed in Table 3.2. It is 1.0 per year, which means that all the carbon stored in litter is replaced each year. Now, the humification factor is 0.4: this indicates that, during a year, 40 per cent of the carbon in the litter store becomes humus; the remaining 60 per cent is respired. So the overall turnover rate for the litter store, k_{56}, is 1.0. When the humification factor is used, this value is automatically adjusted to account for respiratory losses. On the other hand, when a separate note of respiratory losses is required, then we need a rate constant for humification, k_{56}, and a rate constant for respiration, k_{50}. In this case, k_{56} is defined as

$$k_{56} = k_{56} \times h_v$$

and

$$k_{50} = k_{56} \times (1 - h_v)$$

It follows that the sum of the two separate rate constants will be equal to the overall rate constant. By the same token, a carbonization factor, c_v, must be defined to take account of the fact that only part of the carbon released by the humus store enters the stable humus charcoal store: the remainder is respired. The inputs to the stable humus store are thus written:

$$\text{inputs} = c_v(k_{67}x_6)$$

We are now in a position to write the full set of storage equations describing the dynamics of carbon through a terrestrial ecosystem. With account taken of respiratory losses from litter, humus, and stable humus charcoal, it looks like this:

$$\frac{dx_1}{dt} = p_{1,k}z_v - k_{15}x_1$$

$$\frac{dx_2}{dt} = p_{2,k}z_v - k_{25}x_2$$

$$\frac{dx_3}{dt} = p_{3,k}z_v - k_{35}x_3$$

$$\frac{dx_4}{dt} = p_{4,k}z_v - k_{46}x_4$$

$$\frac{dx_5}{dt} = k_{15}x_1 + k_{25}x_2 + k_{35}x_3 - k_{56}x_5 - k_{50}x_5$$

$$\frac{dx_6}{dt} = k_{56}x_5 + k_{46}x_4 - k_{67}x_6 - k_{60}x_6$$

$$\frac{dx_7}{dt} = k_{67}x_6 - k_{70}x_7$$

To render this set of equations operational, we must supply two things: values for the parameters, and starting states for each of the seven state variables. Consider the dynamics of carbon in a tropical forest. Set all state variables to zero. Running the model will then show how the system shifts to its steady state when all the carbon stores start out empty. The value of the driving variable, net primary production, z_1 ($v = 1$, tropical forest), can be gleaned from Table 3.2. It is 27.8 Gt C/yr. The partitioning of this net primary production is determined by the parameters, $p_{i,1}$. For a tropical forest they are $p_{1,1} = 0.3$, $p_{2,1} = 0.2$, $p_{3,1} = 0.3$, and $p_{4,1} = 0.2$ (Table 3.2). The transfer coefficients, k_{ij}, are derived from field data. They, too, are listed in Table 3.2. The parameters used when applying the model to a tropical forest with note taken of respiratory losses from litter, humus, and stable humus charcoal are shown in Fig. 3.5. Expressing time rates of change of

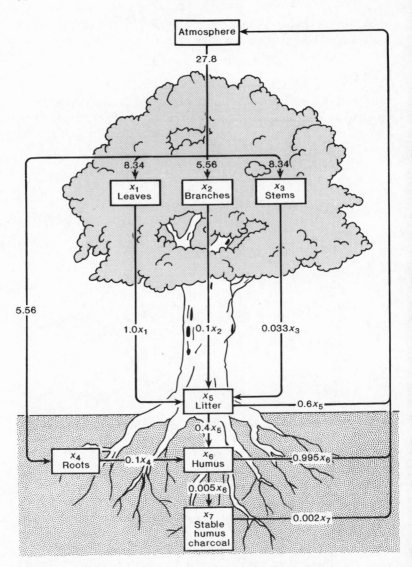

FIG. 3.5. The terrestrial carbon system calibrated for a tropical forest

the state variables as finite difference approximations and adding the relevant parameter values, including transfer coefficients defining respiratory losses from litter, humus, and stable humus charcoal, the calibrated set of equations looks like this:

$$\frac{\Delta x_1}{\Delta t} = (0.3 \times 27.8) - 1.0x_1$$

$$\frac{\Delta x_2}{\Delta t} = (0.2 \times 27.8) - 0.1x_2$$

$$\frac{\Delta x_3}{\Delta t} = (0.3 \times 27.8) - 0.033x_3$$

$$\frac{\Delta x_4}{\Delta t} = (0.2 \times 27.8) - 0.1x_4$$

$$\frac{\Delta x_5}{\Delta t} = 1.0x_1 + 0.1x_2 + 0.033x_3 - 0.4x_5 - 0.6x_5$$

$$\frac{\Delta x_6}{\Delta t} = 0.4x_5 + 0.1x_4 - 0.005x_6 - 0.995x_6$$

$$\frac{\Delta x_7}{\Delta t} = 0.005x_6 - 0.002x_7$$

A solution to this set of equations, with all state variables starting at zero, is shown in Fig. 3.6 (see Box 2). Notice how the carbon stored in plant components rises more rapidly to a steady state than the carbon stored in humus. Carbon stored in stable humus charcoal, with its slow turnover time, changes very sluggishly.

A General Systems Model

In the most general case of a dynamical system model, the time rate of change in any state variable, dx_i/dt, is a function of all other state variables, x_i. It follows that, if a system is fully interconnected, a change in any one state variable will effect a change in all other state variables comprising the system. Such a system may be represented by a set of simultaneous differential equations of the style

$$\frac{dx_1}{dt} = f_1(x_1, x_2, \ldots x_n) + z$$

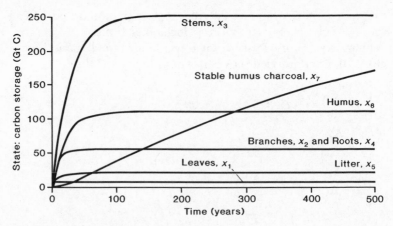

Note: The model assumes that all stores start empty. Notice that most of the state variables attain a steady state within 100 years. The exception is stable humus charcoal which, owing to its slow rate of decay, takes well over 500 years to reach a steady state.

FIG. 3.6. Simulated dynamics of the terrestrial carbon cycle in a tropical forest

BOX 2. *A computer model to simulate the cycle of carbon in terrestrial ecosystems*

This box contains a computer program which will run the model of the terrestrial carbon cycle in the world's chief ecosystems as discussed in the text. Key the program into your computer. To test that it runs correctly, input the data for a tropical forest as listed in Table 3.2. For the sake of convenience, you will be requested to enter the items of data in the same order that they appear in the table. If all be well, the results generated by the program should give the same steady-state values as suggested by Fig. 3.6.

Once bug-free, the program may be used to establish the steady-state storages of carbon in the other ecosystems listed in Table 3.2, namely, temperate forest, grassland, agricultural area, human area, and tundra and semi-desert. You might also examine the effect on steady-state carbon storages of increasing the driving variable by about 10% (a likely consequence of increased carbon dioxide levels in the atmosphere) or of altering the transfer coefficients (e.g. increasing the humification rates by 0.1, 0.2, or even more, figures which might be more representative of a warmer and more humid world).

```
REM
REM Program to simulate the carbon cycle in terrestrial biomes
REM
REM Seven state variables, gigatonnes of carbon stored in:
REM
```

```
REM     leaves              x(1,t)
REM     branches            x(2,t)
REM     stems               x(3,t)
REM     roots               x(4,t)
REM     litter              x(5,t)
REM     humus               x(6,t)
REM     stable humus charcoal x(7,t)
REM
REM Make storage space for 7 state variables and 502 time steps
REM
DIM x(7, 502)
REM
REM Set up initial conditions
REM
10 LET rerun = 0
REM
REM Initialize state variables
FOR i = 1 TO 7
LET x(i, 1) = 0
NEXT i
REM
COLOR 11, 1, 1
CLS
PRINT "Ecosystem reference codes:"
PRINT
PRINT "1 = tropical forest"
PRINT "2 = temperate forest"
PRINT "3 = grassland"
PRINT "4 = agricultural area"
PRINT "5 = human area"
PRINT "6 = tundra and semi-desert"
PRINT
INPUT "Ecosystem type (use the above numerical code) = "; v
IF v = 1 THEN LET biome$ = "tropical forest"
IF v = 2 THEN LET biome$ = "temperate forest"
IF v = 3 THEN LET biome$ = "grassland"
IF v = 4 THEN LET biome$ = "agricultural area"
IF v = 5 THEN LET biome$ = "human area"
IF v = 6 THEN LET biome$ = "tundra and semi-desert"
REM
REM Read area of each ecosystem type (10^12 m^2)
REM
DATA 36.1,17.0,18.8,17.4,2.0,29.7
FOR eco = 1 TO 6
READ area(eco)
NEXT eco
PRINT
PRINT "Enter data:"
PRINT
INPUT "Driving variable, zv (net primary production in Gt C/yr) = "; z
PRINT
PRINT "Partition coefficients, pi,v"
INPUT "Leaves, p1,v = "; p1
INPUT "Branches, p2,v = "; p2
INPUT "Stems, p3,v = "; p3
INPUT "Roots, p4,v = "; p4
PRINT
PRINT "Transfer coefficients, kij"
INPUT "Leaves to litter, k15 = "; k15
INPUT "Branches to litter, k25 = "; k25
INPUT "Stems to litter, k35 = "; k35
INPUT "Roots to humus, k46 = "; k46
INPUT "Litter to humus, k56 = "; k56
INPUT "Humus to charcoal, k67 = "; k67
INPUT "Charcoal to environment, k70 = "; k70
PRINT
INPUT "Humification factor, hv = "; h
INPUT "Carbonization factor, cv = "; c
PRINT
INPUT "Time interval, dt = "; dt
INPUT "How many time steps (maximum 501) "; tt
INPUT "After how many time steps do you wish to program to pause"; pwait
INPUT "Would you prefer the results in Gg (enter 1) or kg/m2 (enter 2)"; units$
INPUT "Do you wish to run with these parameters (y/n)"; go$
```

```
IF go$ = "n" THEN STOP
REM
REM Main computational loop to solve carbon storage equations
REM
FOR t = 1 TO tt
REM
LET x(1, t + 1) = x(1, t) + ((p1 * z) - k15 * x(1, t)) * dt
LET x(2, t + 1) = x(2, t) + ((p2 * z) - k25 * x(2, t)) * dt
LET x(3, t + 1) = x(3, t) + ((p3 * z) - k35 * x(3, t)) * dt
LET x(4, t + 1) = x(4, t) + ((p4 * z) - k46 * x(4, t)) * dt
LET x(5, t + 1) = x(5, t) + (k15 * x(1, t) + k25 * x(2, t) + k35 * x(3, t) - k56 * x(5, t)) * dt
LET x(6, t + 1) = x(6, t) + (h * k46 * x(4, t) + h * k56 * x(5, t) - k67 * x(6, t)) * dt
LET x(7, t + 1) = x(7, t) + (c * k67 * x(6, t) - k70 * x(7, t)) * dt
REM
NEXT t
CLS
REM
REM Print results
REM
PRINT "Terrestrial carbon cycle: the results of a simulation run"
PRINT
PRINT "The ecosystem is "; biome$
PRINT "The time interval is"; dt; "year(s)"
IF units$ = "1" THEN GOTO 30
PRINT "Units are kilogrammes of carbon per square metre (kg C/m^2)"
GOTO 40
30 PRINT "Units are gigatonnes of carbon (Gt C)"
40 PRINT
PRINT
PRINT
PRINT
PRINT " Time    Time  Leaves Branches Stems  Roots  Litter Humus  Charcoal"
PRINT " step    (yr)  x(1,t) x(2,t)  x(3,t) x(4,t) x(5,t) x(6,t) x(7,t) "
PRINT
VIEW PRINT 13 TO 14
LET tc = 0
LET m = 13
FOR t = 1 TO tt
LET tc = tc + 1
IF units$ = "1" THEN GOTO 50
FOR u = 1 TO 6
LET x(u, t) = x(u, t) / area(v)
NEXT u
50 REM
PRINT USING "#####.##"; t - 1; (t - 1) * dt; x(1, t); x(2, t); x(3, t); x(4, t); x(5, t); x(6, t); x(7, t)
IF tc = pwait THEN GOSUB Halt
VIEW PRINT 13 TO 14
IF t = tt THEN GOSUB Finish
NEXT t
IF rerun = 1 THEN GOTO 10
REM
Halt:
VIEW PRINT 16 TO 17
PRINT
PRINT "Press any key to continue"
DO
LOOP WHILE INKEY$ = ""
PRINT
LET tc = 0
RETURN
REM
Finish:
VIEW PRINT 16 TO 18
PRINT
PRINT "Simulation run over. Press any key to continue"
DO
LOOP WHILE INKEY$ = ""
PRINT
INPUT "Have another go (y/n)"; run$
IF run$ = "n" THEN STOP
LET rerun = 1
VIEW PRINT 1 TO 18
RESTORE
RETURN
```

$$\frac{dx_2}{dt} = f_2(x_1, x_2, \ldots x_n) + z$$

$$\ldots$$

$$\frac{dx_n}{dt} = f_n(x_1, x_2, \ldots x_n) + z$$

where the zs stand for driving or forcing variables which act on the system from outside its boundaries (i.e. they are inputs which arrive from outside the system). This set of equations is expressed more succinctly in matrix form as

$$dx/dt = f(x) + z$$

It can be seen that a change in one state variable effects a change in the others. This demonstrates in mathematical terms the fact that, through the interrelations among its components, a system acts as a single unit. As so lucidly shown by Ludwig von Bertalanffy (1951; 1973), systems of equations of this kind are found in many fields, the measures used to define the state variables varying from one application to another. The general stability conditions of the equations can be found by methods which, although beyond the scope of this book, are well tried and tested (see May, 1973; Puccia and Levins, 1985).

Spatial Systems

In many environmental systems, the behaviour of processes in space is of paramount interest. The same general state equations can be used in this case, but an extra term must be added to allow for spatial variations in the state variables. For state variable x_i, the state equation would be of the form

$$\frac{\delta x_i}{\delta t} = f_i(x, z) + \nabla \cdot (D_i \nabla x_i)$$

where ∇ denotes spatial gradients (along the x, y, and z directions).

To clarify all this, let us take a close look at a simple spatial model of nitrogen movement in a catchment. Basically, all that is required for the conversion of a non-spatial model to a spatial model is to disaggregate the state variables among a set of spatial units such as grid-cells. The modification can be done by adding labels to the terms in the storage equations which, like map co-ordinates, indicate locations in a spatial domain. A catchment

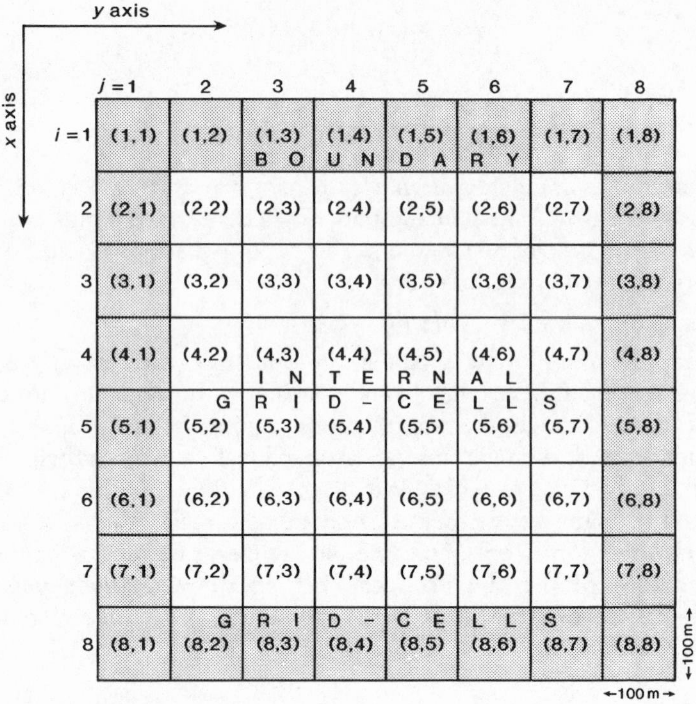

Note: The x and y axes are spatial co-ordinates used to locate each grid-cell, as grid references are employed to locate features on a map.

FIG. 3.7. A two-dimensional spatial grid dividing the spatial domain of the system into grid-cells

occupies a three-dimensional domain. We shall simplify the situation by ignoring the differences in nitrogen storage at different depths in the soil, and use a two-dimensional grid dividing the catchment into a set of grid-cells (Fig. 3.7). Positions within this domain may be referred to by horizontal x and y co-ordinates. The nitrogen balance for grid-cell i, j may be expressed as:

$$\begin{array}{l} \text{nitrogen stored} \\ \text{in grid-cell } i, j \\ \text{at time } t + 1 \end{array} = \begin{array}{l} \text{nitrogen stored in grid-cell} \\ i, j \text{ at time } t \end{array}$$

$$+ \left(\begin{array}{l} \text{nitrogen} \\ \text{inputs to} \\ \text{grid-cell } i, j \end{array} - \begin{array}{l} \text{nitrogen} \\ \text{outputs from} \\ \text{grid-cell } i, j \end{array} \right) \Delta t$$

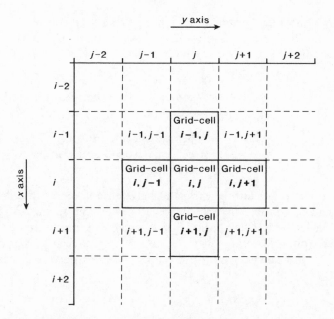

Note: In the model of nitrogen storage and transfer, the grid-cells lying north $(i - 1, j)$, south $(i + 1, j)$, east $(i, j + 1)$, and west $(i, j - 1)$ are used. Other applications might involve the use of grid-cells lying diagonally adjacent $(i - 1, j - 1; i - 1, j + 1; i + 1, j - 1; i + 1, j + 1)$ to grid-cell i, j.

FIG. 3.8. Grid-cell i, j and adjacent grid-cells

In a spatial system, the transfers of matter depend upon the spatial pattern of the state variables and upon any spatial variations in the values of the rate constants or other parameters. Consequently, transport laws in a spatial model must include spatial terms. Nitrogen is transferred from one grid-cell to another by water movement. As a crude approximation, let us assume that the downslope rate of nitrogen transfer between grid-cells is proportional to the negative-slope gradient between adjacent cells:

$$\begin{array}{ll} \text{downslope} \\ \text{nitrogen transfer} \end{array} = \begin{array}{l} \text{negative-slope} \\ \text{gradient} \end{array} \times \begin{array}{l} \text{nitrogen storage} \\ \text{in grid-cell } i, j \end{array}$$

Now, grid-cell i, j lies adjacent to four other grid-cells: cell $i - 1, j$, cell $i + 1, j$, cell $i, j - 1$, and cell $i, j + 1$ (Fig. 3.8). Water may move across any of the faces between these grid-cells. In addition, rainfall will add nitrogen to each grid-cell. So, a full nitrogen-storage equation for grid-cell i, j looks like this:

$$\begin{pmatrix} \text{nitrogen stored} \\ \text{in grid-cell} \\ i, j \text{ at time } t + 1 \end{pmatrix} = \begin{pmatrix} \text{nitrogen stored} \\ \text{in grid-cell} \\ i, j \text{ at time } t \end{pmatrix} + \begin{pmatrix} \text{nitrogen transfer} \\ \text{between grid-cells} \\ i, j \text{ and } i - 1, j \end{pmatrix}$$

$$+ \begin{pmatrix} \text{nitrogen transfer} \\ \text{between grid-cells} \\ i, j \text{ and } i + 1, j \end{pmatrix} + \begin{pmatrix} \text{nitrogen transfer} \\ \text{between grid-cells} \\ i, j \text{ and } i, j - 1 \end{pmatrix}$$

$$+ \begin{pmatrix} \text{nitrogen transfer} \\ \text{between grid-cells} \\ i, j \text{ and } i, j + 1 \end{pmatrix} + \begin{pmatrix} \text{nitrogen} \\ \text{added in} \\ \text{rainfall} \end{pmatrix} \Delta t$$

The direction of nitrogen transfer between adjacent grid-cells will depend upon the difference in elevation between them. Plainly, if grid-cell $i - 1, j$ lies upslope of grid-cell i, j, then nitrogen will move from grid-cell $i - 1, j$ to grid-cell i, j. Conversely, if grid-cell $i - 1, j$ lies downslope of grid-cell i, j, then nitrogen will move in

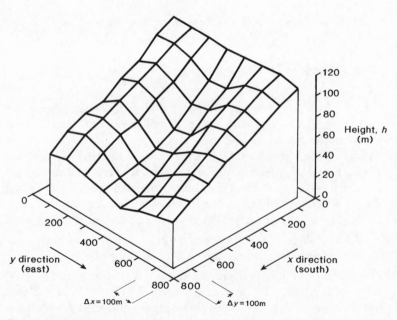

FIG. 3.9. The topography of the 8 × 8 spatial domain to which the nitrogen storage and transfer model is applied

BOX 3. *A computer model to simulate the dynamics of soil nitrogen in a catchment*

This box contains a computer program that will run the model of soil nitrogen storage and transfer in a catchment as discussed in the text. To test the program once you have keyed it into your computer, simply run it and input the following data when requested so to do: initial nitrogen content of grid-cells = 5000; nitrogen input in rainfall = 16; time interval of integration = 0.1; total number of time steps = 101. The results should give the same pattern of nitrogen storage as shown for years 1 and 10 in Fig. 3.10. Take care when typing the minus signs in the equations for the boundary grid-cells, or you might find that nitrogen moves up-hill!

The program is long. Much of it is taken up by statements specifying the conditions at the boundaries (edges and corners) of the spatial domain. The working core of the program, which solves the storage equations by the Euler method, is relatively short. The flow chart depicted in Fig. 1.4 gives the main sequence of computations in the program, though this flow chart refers to the author's own version of the program and not the 'user-friendly' version developed for this book.

Once the program is free of errors, you might experiment with different initial concentrations of nitrogen and different nitrogen inputs in rainfall. Also, you might devise your own catchment by changing the DATA statements defining the elevations of grid-cells. Providing there are 8 × 8 elevations, the program should produce sensible results. You could, if you wish, alter the horizontal dimensions of the grid-cells by changing the values of *dx* and *dy* in the program. Appropriate changes would need to be made in some of the PRINT statements where, at present, distances east and south are expressed in hundreds of metres.

As the model stands, nitrogen gains and losses in each grid-cell will eventually balance one another. Once such a balance is attained, the storage of nitrogen will stay constant indefinitely. In the example, this steady state is reached in about 800 years, and is very like the state after 100 years (Fig. 3.10). In reality, some nitrogen will be held in the soil and some in the vegetation. This 'immobile' store of nitrogen could be included in the model by adding a term for it, *nsv*. Basically, the nitrogen store in a grid-cell will not fall below the value of *nsv*. To ensure that this condition be complied with, the line preventing the nitrogen content of a grid-cell from becoming negative, which appears after the main nitrogen storage equation, should be amended to read:

IF $n(2, i, j) < nsv$ THEN LET $n(2, i, j) = nsv + nrain*dt$

nsv would need defining somewhere in the program. A term for nitrogen removed by cropping, *ncrop*, could be included as follows:

LET $n(2, i, j) = n(1, i, j) + ((e1 + e2 + e3 + e4)*dt)$
$+ (nrain*dt) - (ncrop*dt)$

```
REM
REM A model to simulate the flux of nitrogen in a catchment
REM
COLOR 11, 1, 1
CLS
PRINT "A simulation of soil nitrogen dynamics in a catchment"
PRINT
REM
```

```
REM Elevations, h, in metres for each grid-cell
REM
DATA 105,105,105,104,106,108,110,108
DATA 98,100,96,94,96,100,104,100
DATA 82,90,82,80,85,90,95,90
DATA 75,82,75,56,60,80,85,80
DATA 62,74,62,46,52,64,72,74
DATA 60,66,60,42,40,52,62,62
DATA 52,60,52,38,30,40,50,55
DATA 40,45,40,36,28,36,40,45
REM
LET ii = 8
LET jj = 8
FOR i = 1 TO ii
FOR j = 1 TO jj
READ h(i, j)
NEXT j
NEXT i
INPUT "Display elevation data (y/n)"; prin$
IF prin$ <> "y" THEN GOTO 10
CLS 0
PRINT "Elevation of grid-cells (metres)"
PRINT
PRINT "     100 200 300 400 500 600 700 800 Distance east (m) "
PRINT
FOR i = 1 TO ii
PRINT USING "#####"; i * 100; h(i, 1); h(i, 2); h(i, 3); h(i, 4); h(i, 5); h(i, 6); h(i, 7); h(i, 8)
PRINT
NEXT i
PRINT " Distance south (m)"
GOSUB Keywait
10 REM
REM Grid-cell types
REM
DATA 6,2,2,2,2,2,2,7
DATA 5,1,1,1,1,1,1,3
DATA 5,1,1,1,1,1,1,3
DATA 5,1,1,1,1,1,1,3
DATA 5,1,1,1,1,1,1,3
DATA 5,1,1,1,1,1,1,3
DATA 5,1,1,1,1,1,1,3
DATA 9,4,4,4,4,4,4,8
REM
FOR i = 1 TO ii
FOR j = 1 TO jj
READ cell(i, j)
NEXT j
NEXT i
REM
REM Compute slope gradients, dh/dx and dh/dy, for each grid-cell
REM
REM dx and dy are the lengths of the grid-cell edges in metres
REM
LET dx = 100
LET dy = 100
REM
FOR i = 1 TO ii
FOR j = 1 TO jj
LET c = cell(i, j)
REM
REM Central cells
REM
IF c <> 1 THEN GOTO 200
LET s1(i, j) = -(h(i, j) - h(i + 1, j)) / dx
LET s2(i, j) = -(h(i, j) - h(i - 1, j)) / dx
LET s3(i, j) = -(h(i, j) - h(i, j + 1)) / dy
LET s4(i, j) = -(h(i, j) - h(i, j - 1)) / dy
GOTO 1000
REM
REM Northern boundary cells
REM
200 IF c <> 2 THEN GOTO 300
LET s1(1, j) = -(h(1, j) - h(2, j)) / dx
```

```
LET s2(1, j) = s1(1, j)
LET s3(1, j) = -(h(1, j) - h(1, j + 1)) / dy
LET s4(1, j) = -(h(1, j) - h(1, j - 1)) / dy
GOTO 1000
REM
REM Eastern boundary cells
REM
300 IF c <> 3 THEN GOTO 400
LET s1(i, 8) = -(h(i, 8) - h(i + 1, 8)) / dx
LET s2(i, 8) = -(h(i, 8) - h(i - 1, 8)) / dx
LET s4(i, 8) = -(h(i, 8) - h(i, 7)) / dy
LET s3(i, 8) = -s4(i, 8)
GOTO 1000
REM
REM Southern boundary cells
REM
400 IF c <> 4 THEN GOTO 500
LET s2(8, j) = -(h(8, j) - h(7, j)) / dx
LET s1(8, j) = -s2(8, j)
LET s3(8, j) = -(h(8, j) - h(8, j + 1)) / dy
LET s4(8, j) = -(h(8, j) - h(8, j - 1)) / dy
GOTO 1000
REM
REM Western boundary cells
REM
500 IF c <> 5 THEN GOTO 600
LET s1(i, 1) = -(h(i, 1) - h(i + 1, 1)) / dx
LET s2(i, 1) = -(h(i, 1) - h(i - 1, 1)) / dx
LET s3(i, 1) = -(h(i, 1) - h(i, 2)) / dy
LET s4(i, 1) = -s3(i, 1)
GOTO 1000
REM
REM Northwestern corner cell
REM
600 IF c <> 6 THEN GOTO 700
LET s1(1, 1) = -(h(1, 1) - h(2, 1)) / dx
LET s2(1, 1) = s1(1, 1)
LET s3(1, 1) = -(h(1, 1) - h(1, 2)) / dy
LET s4(1, 1) = s3(1, 1)
GOTO 1000
REM
REM Northeastern corner cell
REM
700 IF c <> 7 THEN GOTO 800
LET s1(1, 8) = -(h(1, 8) - h(2, 8)) / dx
LET s2(1, 8) = s1(1, 8)
LET s4(1, 8) = -(h(1, 8) - h(1, 7)) / dy
LET s3(1, 8) = -s4(1, 8)
GOTO 1000
REM
REM Southeastern corner cell
REM
800 IF c <> 8 THEN GOTO 900
LET s2(8, 8) = -(h(8, 8) - h(7, 8)) / dx
LET s1(8, 8) = -s2(8, 8)
LET s4(8, 8) = -(h(8, 8) - h(8, 7)) / dy
LET s3(8, 8) = -s4(8, 8)
GOTO 1000
REM
REM Southwestern corner cell
REM
900 REM
LET s2(8, 1) = -(h(8, 1) - h(7, 1)) / dx
LET s1(8, 1) = -s2(8, 1)
LET s3(8, 1) = -(h(8, 1) - h(8, 2)) / dy
LET s4(8, 1) = -s3(8, 1)
1000 REM
NEXT j
NEXT i
REM
REM Initialize grid-cell nitrogen contents
REM
9999 LET rerun = 0
```

```
CLS 0
VIEW PRINT 1 TO 10
INPUT "Initial nitrogen content of grid-cells (kg/ha) = "; n0
FOR i = 1 TO i
FOR j = 1 TO jj
LET n(1, i, j) = n0
LET n(2, i, j) = 0
NEXT j
NEXT i
REM
REM Nitrogen in rainfall
REM
INPUT "Nitrogen input in rainfall (kg/ha.yr) = "; nrain
REM
REM Enter time interval of integration
REM
INPUT "Time interval, dt (years) (0.1 recommended) = "; dt
REM
INPUT "Total number of time steps = "; tt
REM
INPUT "How often do you wish the program to pause (time steps)"; tp
PRINT
INPUT "Do wish to run with these parameters (y/n)"; go$
IF go$ = "n" THEN STOP
CLS
REM
REM Display results
REM
LET year = 0
LET tc = 0
LET tprin = 0
REM
CLS
999 REM Main loop for solving system equations
IF rerun = 1 THEN GOTO 9999
VIEW PRINT 1 TO 22
PRINT "Time step:"; tc; "    Year:"; year
PRINT
PRINT "        100   200   300   400   500   600   700   800  y (m)"
PRINT
FOR i = 1 TO 8
FOR j = 1 TO 8
LET nn(i, j) = n(1, i, j)
NEXT j
NEXT i
FOR i = 1 TO ii
PRINT USING "########"; i * 100; INT(nn(i, 1)); INT(nn(i, 2)); INT(nn(i, 3)); INT(nn(i, 4)); INT(nn(i, 5));
INT(nn(i, 6)); INT(nn(i, 7)); INT(nn(i, 8))
PRINT
NEXT i
PRINT "   x (m)"
IF tc = 0 OR tprin = tp THEN GOSUB Keywait
30 REM
REM
REM Storage equations
REM
FOR i = 1 TO ii
FOR j = 1 TO jj
IF s1(i, j) <= 0 THEN LET e1 = s1(i, j) * n(1, i, j)
IF s1(i, j) > 0 THEN LET e1 = s1(i, j) * n(1, i + 1, j)
IF s2(i, j) <= 0 THEN LET e2 = s2(i, j) * n(1, i, j)
IF s2(i, j) > 0 THEN LET e2 = s2(i, j) * n(1, i - 1, j)
IF s3(i, j) <= 0 THEN LET e3 = s3(i, j) * n(1, i, j)
IF s3(i, j) > 0 THEN LET e3 = s3(i, j) * n(1, i, j + 1)
IF s4(i, j) <= 0 THEN LET e4 = s4(i, j) * n(1, i, j)
IF s4(i, j) > 0 THEN LET e4 = s4(i, j) * n(1, i, j - 1)
REM
LET n(2, i, j) = n(1, i, j) + ((e1 + e2 + e3 + e4) * dt) + (nrain * dt)
REM
IF n(2, i, j) < 0 THEN LET n(2, i, j) = 0 + nrain * dt
NEXT j
NEXT i
```

```
LET tc = tc + 1
LET tprin = tprin + 1
LET year = tc * dt
REM
REM Overwrite time steps 1 and 2
REM
FOR i = 1 TO ii
FOR j = 1 TO jj
LET n(1, i, j) = n(2, i, j)
NEXT j
NEXT i
IF tc = tt THEN GOSUB Finish
GOTO 999
REM
Keywait:
VIEW PRINT 24 TO 25
PRINT "Press any key when ready to resume run"
DO
LOOP WHILE INKEY$ = ""
PRINT
LET tprin = 0
RETURN
REM
Finish:
VIEW PRINT 24 TO 25
PRINT "Simulation run over. Press any key to continue"
DO
LOOP WHILE INKEY$ = ""
PRINT
INPUT "Have another go (y/n)"; run$
IF run$ = "n" THEN STOP
LET rerun = 1
CLS
PRINT "A simulation of soil nitrogen dynamics in a catchment"
PRINT
RETURN
```

the opposite direction, from grid-cell i, j to grid-cell $i - 1$, j. Special accounting procedures need defining for the grid-cells at the edge of the catchment; these are known as the boundary conditions.

By way of illustration, the model was programmed to predict the changing nitrogen storage in an 8×8 set of grid-cells, each 1 ha in area, with the topography shown in Fig. 3.9 (see Box 3). For simplicity, soil depth was assumed constant over the spatial domain of the system. Initial nitrogen storage was set at 5000 kg/ha in all grid-cells. Nitrogen was assumed to enter the system in precipitation at a rate of 16 kg/ha/yr. The rate constants of nitrogen transfer between adjacent grid-cells were defined as the tangent of the slope between the grid-cells, the direction of transfer depending on which of the grid-cells lay upslope. Changing nitrogen storages over a 100-year period were simulated using a time

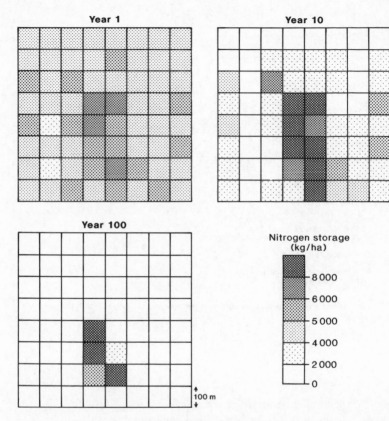

Note: A time interval of 0.1 yr was used in the simulations. Predicted nitrogen storage (kg/ha) is shown for years 1, 10, and 100.

FIG. 3.10. Simulated changes of nitrogen storage over the 8 × 8 spatial domain depicted in Fig. 3.9

interval of $\Delta t = 0.1$ years. The predictions for 1, 10, and 100 years are portrayed in Fig. 3.10. The depletion of nitrogen on summits and nose-slopes, and its accumulation in valley-bottom sites, is evident. More sophisticated models of this kind are being developed to simulate nutrient dynamics in landscapes (e.g. Bartell and Brenkert, 1991). The use of a regular grid facilitates calibration by means of remotely sensed data on topography, soils, and vegetation.

We are now armed with enough background information on mathematical models to embark on a survey of actual examples of environmental problems which have been investigated using modelling techniques.

Part II
Practice

4

Energy Balances

Human activities are changing the composition of the atmosphere. The changes are occurring chiefly in the gaseous component, but the dust burden is increasing, too. They threaten to have quite radical repercussions on the state of the world climate system by altering the energy balance of the Earth–atmosphere system. This chapter will consider three topics concerned with the climatic consequences of human activities: models used to predict the plausible effects of increased greenhouse gases in the air; models used to simulate the climatic consequences of a major nuclear exchange between the superpowers; and models used to investigate the effects on the climate system of the burning Kuwait oil wells. The nuclear exchange models, though it is to be hoped they will be of purely academic interest, also throw light on the likely consequences of large asteroid strikes or the supereruption of volcanoes charged with a high proportion of sulphur volatiles. Before proceeding to examine these topics, it may be salutary to outline the rather complicated models used to simulate changes in the world climate system.

Climate Models

The models used to simulate the chemical reactions and physical processes in the atmosphere are exceedingly sophisticated. There is little point here in delving too deeply into their workings, since the novice modeller would be hard pressed to digest and assimilate the complexities of atmospheric physics and chemistry. Suffice it to outline the chief types of model, describe their basic components, and summarize the ways in which they are used.

Kinds of Climate Model

A range of climate models have been built in recent decades, varying from simple zero-dimensional models to far more elaborate three-dimensional models. Four chief types of climate model now exist. Energy balance models (EBMs) predict the change in temperature at the surface of the Earth in response to a change in heating, with the proviso that the net flux of energy remain unchanged. The biggest drawback with EBMs is that they do not include a physically based model of the atmosphere. Next are radiative-convective models (RCMs). These compute the vertical (one-dimensional) temperature profile of a single column of air. Normally, the predicted temperatures are global averages. In general, because they deal with 'average' conditions and their results are strongly influenced by the assumptions made about cloud feedback, surface albedo, and so forth, RCMs are not particularly trustworthy. Statistical dynamical models (SDMs) normally deal with a two-dimensional slice of air along a line, commonly a line of latitude. They thus combine the latitudinal dimension of EBMs with the vertical dimension of RCMs. A set of statistics is used to specify wind speeds and directions (hence the designation 'statistical' models). Useful though they can be, SDMs fail to resolve zonal differences within the climate system.

General circulation models (GCMs), the most sophisticated climate models currently available, tackle three-dimensional parcels of air as they move horizontally and vertically through the atmosphere. They are not limited by explicit spatial averaging. Their chief restrictions are the long computing times and the paucity of adequate data with which to calibrate them. There are three types of GCM: atmospheric general circulation models (AGCMs), which predict the state of the atmosphere; oceanic general circulation models (OGCMs), which predict the state of the oceans and range from simple, mixed-layer ocean to full-ocean general circulation models; and coupled atmosphere–ocean general circulation models (AOGCMs), which, as their name hints, consider the atmosphere and ocean simultaneously. When atmosphere and ocean models are coupled, the grid size is, perforce, coarse (even the fastest and largest computers cannot at present handle the amount of information in coupled models at a very high level of resolution), and they are very costly to run. The chief physical processes and interactions, and the spatial structure, of a coupled atmosphere–ocean model is set down in Fig. 4.1.

A Basic General Circulation Model

A GCM consists of a set of equations describing the physical and dynamical processes which determine climate. These equations are

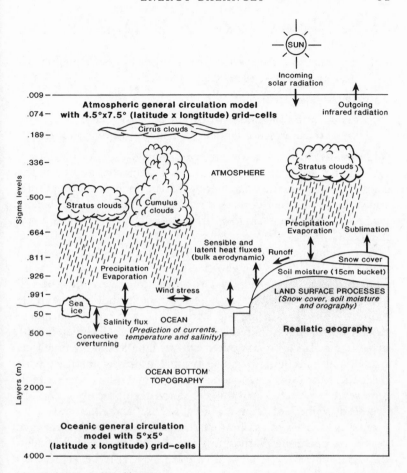

After Washington and Meehl (1991).

FIG. 4.1. A schematic diagram of a coupled atmosphere–ocean general circulation model showing the vertical structure of atmospheric and oceanic layers and the chief physical process and interactions modelled

prognostic, that is, they enable predictions about the state of the atmosphere (or ocean) to be made. Additionally, many GCMs include a heat-and-water-balance model of the land surface, and a mixed-layer model of the ocean. At the heart of a GCM lie the governing or primitive equations:

1. the equation of motion (conservation of momentum);
2. the equation of continuity (conservation of mass or hydro-dynamic equation);

3. the equation of continuity for atmospheric water vapour (conservation of water vapour); and
4. the equation of energy (thermodynamic equation derived from the first law of thermodynamics).

To these storage equations are added:

5. the equation of state (hydrostatic equation); and
6. the surface pressure tendency equation (in some models).

Additionally, to use a GCM, it is necessary to specify parameters such as the solar constant and orbital parameters, and boundary conditions such as the distribution of land and sea, topography, and total atmospheric mass and composition. GCMs include diagnostic variables—clouds, surface albedo, vertical velocity, and the like.

At present, the smallest spatial unit used in GCMs is a grid-cell about 100×100 km. Diagnostic variables, such as clouds, result from processes operating at a smaller scale than the grid-cell. Processes going on within a grid-cell can be included in the model indirectly by representing the state of the grid-cell as parameter values. For instance, individual clouds cannot be included directly in GCMs because no computer can yet handle small enough cell sizes to take account of cloud-forming processes, at least when the entire globe is being modelled. However, cloudiness can be represented by a few parameters derived empirically from cell-averaged values of temperature, winds, and humidity. This process is referred to as parameterization. Biological and chemical processes operating within a grid-cell, which clearly influence the atmospheric system as a whole, may also be represented parametrically.

For prescribed boundary conditions and parameters, the full set of equations is solved to determine the rates of change in prognostic variables such as temperature, surface pressure, horizontal velocity, water vapour, and soil moisture. There is no doubt that state-of-the-art AGCMs and coupled atmosphere–ocean GCMs are complicated, but they are powerful and sophisticated tools in modelling the human impact on several environmental systems. They allow, for example, predictions to be made of future atmospheric states given inputs of several constituents, each of which changes with time, and have, therefore, proved invaluable in assessing the credible degree and pattern of warming associated with the release of greenhouse gases by human activities, as we shall now see.

Modelling Global Warming

There is good observational evidence that the concentrations of some atmospheric gases are on the increase owing to emissions from human population, settlements, fossil-fuel consumption, agricultural practices, and industry. Gases on the increase include carbon dioxide (CO_2), carbon monoxide (CO), methane (CH_4), nitrous oxide (N_2O), nitrogen oxides (NO_x), and chlorofluoro-carbons (CFCs). The annual rate of increase of carbon dioxide is 0.5 per cent, methane 0.9 per cent, nitrous oxide 0.25 per cent, and CFCs 0.4 per cent.

A Warmer, More Humid World

Almost without exception, models which simulate the effect of much higher burdens of carbon dioxide and trace gases in the atmosphere predict that the Earth will be a warmer and more humid planet. The temperature rise could lie in the range 1–5 °C, if the carbon dioxide concentration were to double. The basic reasons for the increased temperature and humidity are not difficult to grasp. The higher the concentration of greenhouse gases in the atmosphere, the greater the amount of infra-red radiation emitted from the Earth's surface absorbed by atmosphere, and so the hotter the atmosphere. With a warmer atmosphere, evaporation of water from the world's oceans increases, so leading to a more vigorous pumping of water round the hydrological cycle. This results in an increased occurrence of droughts and of very wet conditions, the last created by deeper thunderstorms with greater rainfall (Hansen et al., 1991). Tropical cyclones also become more destructive. The increased humidity of the air may itself boost greenhouse warming, since water vapour absorbs infra-red radiation.

Climate models predict an uneven warming of the atmosphere, the poles warming far more than the tropics (Table 4.1). This differential warming is predicted to alter substantially the global pattern of evaporation and precipitation and to cause radical changes of climate in most regions outside the tropical zone. The potential changes of climate are predicted to be greater than most

TABLE 4.1. *General character of results of model simulations by geographical domains*

	Highly likely	Likely	Possible
Global domain	An equilibrium temperature sensitivity of 1 to 5°C for a CO_2 doubling (or equivalent) The rate of climatic warming will accelerate with continuing increases in greenhouse gas emissions Rates of evaporation and precipitation will increase The stratosphere will cool Equilibrium warming will be greatest in high latitudes and lowest in the tropics	The warming of land areas will occur in advance of the warming of ocean areas	The intensity of precipitation will increase
High latitudes	Initially, warming will be greatest in late autumn or winter and spring, but as greenhouse gas concentrations continue to rise, so warming will become greatest in mid-winter	Sea ice will retreat	Warming will be delayed owing to changes in the circulation patterns of the oceans

Middle latitudes	Warming will be least in summer Soil moisture contents and runoff rates will increase owing to a year-round increase of precipitation Summertime evaporation rates will increase owing to increased warming	Precipitation in winter and spring will increase and will lead to increased soil moisture levels in spring	Soil moisture will decrease in summer
Low latitudes	The temperature increase will be less than the global average temperature increase	Precipitation changes in the dry subtropics will, in general, be small with large areas of reduced precipitation The zonal mean precipitation of the tropics will increase, but the extra precipitation will be unevenly distributed The temperaature will increase relatively uniformly throughout the year	The frequency or intensity (or both) of tropical cyclones will increase

After MacCracken et al. (1991: table 1, p. 586).

changes of global climate during the last two million years. The speed with which these climatic changes will occur is open to question. The big unknown is the extent to which the oceans, which, with a high thermal capacity, can absorb enormous amounts of heat, will moderate the increase in atmospheric temperatures. Attempts to gauge the role of the oceans have been made using coupled atmosphere–ocean GCMs (Washington and Meehl, 1991). In one set of experiments, it was found that the response of the atmosphere to increased carbon dioxide concentrations depended on the type of ocean model employed (simple mixed-layer model and coarse-grid ocean GCM) and on the kind of carbon dioxide forcing involved (an instantaneous doubling of atmospheric carbon dioxide from 330 to 660 ppm and a gradually rising—transient—increase starting at 330 ppm and increasing at a rate of 1 per cent a year). For instance, with instantaneous doubling of atmospheric carbon dioxide levels, the mixed-layer ocean model produced a globally average surface air temperature increase of 3.5 °C, whereas the coarse-grid ocean model produced a 1.6 °C rise.

Control Measures

A major effort to evaluate the effects of rising concentrations of greenhouse gases is being made by the Intergovernmental Panel on Climate Change (IPCC). As part of this project, scenarios have been devised to cover possible emissions of carbon dioxide, carbon monoxide, methane, nitrous oxide, nitrogen oxides, and chlorofluorocarbons from the present to the year 2100. In all scenarios, the growth of the world economy and world population was assumed to be the same: population was assumed to climb to 10.5 billion in the second half of the twenty-first century; the world economy was assumed to grow annually at a rate of 2–3 per cent in the OECD countries, and at a rate of 3–5 per cent in Eastern Europe and developing countries, during the 1990s, and to decline somewhat thereafter. Four scenarios were devised (Fig. 4.2). Scenario A, the business-as-usual scenario, assumes on the energy production side intensive use of coal and, on the demand side, only modest efficiency increases. Carbon monoxide controls are moderate, deforestation continues unbridled, and agricultural emissions of methane and nitrous oxide are uncontrolled. The Montreal Protocol for CFC emissions is implemented,

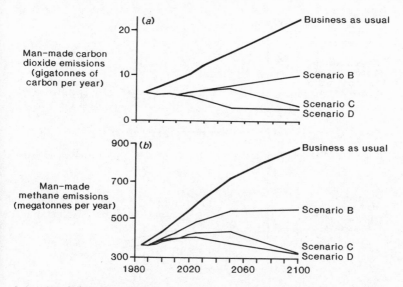

Source: Houghton *et al.* (1990: fig. on p. xxxiv).

FIG. 4.2. Emissions of (*a*) carbon dioxide and (*b*) methane to the year 2100 caused by human activities in the four scenarios developed by the IPCC Working Group III

but with only partial participation. Scenario B assumes, on the production side, a shift towards the use of lower-carbon fuels, notably natural gas, and, on the demand side, significant efficiency increases. Carbon monoxide controls are stringent, deforestation is reversed, and the Montreal Protocol is adhered to by all participants. Scenario C envisages a shift towards renewable energy use and nuclear energy in the second half of the next century. CFCs are phased out and agricultural emissions limited. In Scenario D, the shift to renewable energy use and nuclear energy takes place in the first half of the next century, so reducing the emissions of carbon dioxide. Under this scenario, stringent controls in industrialized countries and moderate growth of emissions in developing countries could stabilize atmospheric carbon dioxide concentrations.

The future atmospheric concentrations of carbon dioxide, methane, and CFC-11 which would result from the four different emission scenarios are shown in Fig. 4.3. The effects that these

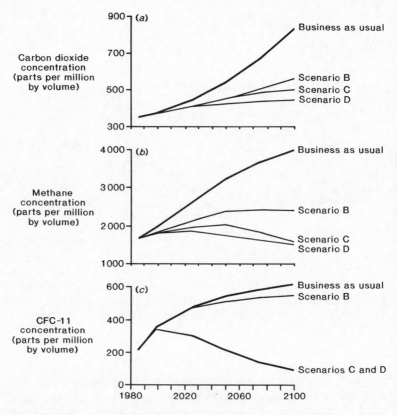

Source: Houghton *et al.* (1990: fig. 5, p. xix).

FIG. 4.3. Atmospheric concentrations of carbon dioxide, methane, and CFC-11 resulting from the four IPCC emissions scenarios

increased greenhouse gas concentrations would have on future global temperatures were simulated using a box-diffusion-upwelling ocean–atmosphere climate model. This 'simple' model translates the greenhouse forcing into temperature change. Where possible, it was calibrated against more complex coupled atmosphere–ocean GCMs. The results (Fig. 4.4) predict that, under the business-as-usual scenario, global mean temperatures will rise during the next century at a rate of about 0.3 °C per decade. The result would be a global mean temperature some 4 °C above its pre-industrial level by the close of the next century.

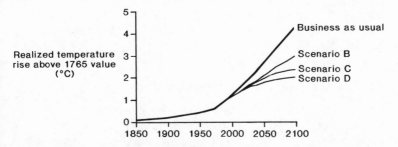

Source: Houghton et al. (1990, fig. 9, p. xxiii).

FIG. 4.4. Simulations of the increase in global mean temperature 1850–1990 due to observed increases in greenhouse gases, and predictions of the rise resulting from the IPCC scenarios

Under the scenarios in which controls on emissions are assumed, global mean temperatures still rise, but at a lower rate—some 0.2 °C per decade in Scenario B, and 0.1 °C for Scenarios C and D. (For the latest IPCC emissions scenarios, see Houghton et al., 1992.)

Natural Causes of Climatic Change

It cannot be over-stressed that all current observations of global change must be set in the context of natural cycles in the biosphere and geosphere (cf. Schlesinger, 1991: 9). The present increase of carbon dioxide in the atmosphere is, almost certainly, an unusual event produced by human activity. Indeed, Thomas J. Crowley (1991: 42), having investigated past geological analogues of the present situation, believes that future greenhouse warming could well create a climate unique in Earth's history. A consequence of more carbon dioxide in the atmosphere is a general warming of the globe. But natural cycles of climatic change may also lead to fluctuations in atmospheric carbon dioxide levels, and so to general warming and cooling of the atmosphere. Global warming induced by human activities (largely the burning of fossil fuels and deforestation) must be evaluated against the background of these natural climatic cycles. The latest work suggests that the effects of natural solar variability are unlikely significantly to alter the warming associated with greenhouse gases as projected for the next century (e.g. Hoffert, 1991). Volcanic (and, to a lesser extent, industrial and domestic) emissions of sulphur volatiles may delay some of the temperature rise, for, combined with water, sulphur forms tiny droplets of sulphuric acid which reflect sunlight (Wigley, 1989; 1992).

The Climatic Consequences of Nuclear War

After the first nuclear explosions over Nagasaki and Hiroshima in August 1945, it was realized that multiple detonations could wreak horrendous destruction on people and their cultures. Not until the mid-1970s did concern grow over the long-term consequences of nuclear war, over the effects on the life and life-support systems of the biosphere. What would a nuclear war do to the air, water, and soils? What effect would it have on animals and plants? The study of long-term effects of nuclear war on the environment shifted into top gear in 1982 when several organizations and individual scientists launched fresh explorations of anticipated global effects. Groups involved in these pioneering projects included the American Association for the Advancement of Science, the United States National Academy of Sciences, and the World Health Organization. Also in 1982, an influential paper was published in the journal *Ambio* by Paul J. Crutzen and John W. Birks (1982). Originally intending to look at the possible effects of nuclear war on the ozone layer, these researchers made the startling new suggestion that, while ozone changes might not be inappreciable, the pall of smoke and soot (and to a lesser extent dust) created by burning cities and forests after a nuclear exchange would so reduce the amount of light reaching the Earth's surface that profound changes in weather would take place. There would, literally, be 'twilight at noon'.

Initial Predictions: Nuclear Winters

Spurred on by the Crutzen and Birks paper, a group of American scientists set about modelling the long-term effects of a nuclear war. The group comprised Richard P. Turco, Owen B. Toon, Thomas P. Ackerman, James B. Pollock, and Carl Sagan. It projected that the pall of dust, smoke, and soot arising in the aftermath of a nuclear exchange would have atmospheric effects that, far from being confined to the blast zone, would change climate on a hemispherical, and even global, scale (see Turco *et al.*, 1983; Ehrlich *et al.*, 1984). The projections were made using mathematical models. Three models were employed: a nuclear-war scenario model; a particle microphysics model; and a radiative-convective climate model. The nuclear-war scenario model predicted, for given assumptions about the megatonnage, fission yield fractions, and location and heights of detonations, the altitudinal distribution of injections of dust, smoke, radioactivity, and nitrogen oxides. The one-dimensional microphysical model predicted the dynamics of the dust and smoke clouds. And the one-dimensional radiative-convective model used the computed dust and smoke particle size, in conjunction with suitable optical coefficients derived from Mie theory (see Pittock et al., 1986: 70), to calculate visible and infra-red optical properties, light fluxes, and air temperatures as a function of time and height. Several scenarios were devised, each assuming different levels of mega-tonnage, sites of detonations, and the nature of detonations (airbursts or ground bursts) (Table 4.2).

The results of the simulations for the different scenarios are summarized in Fig. 4.5. Predictions represent effects averaged over the northern hemisphere. The initial nuclear explosions and fires are located in the northern mid-latitudes in a zone between 30° to 60° N. However, within days the entire northern hemisphere suffers a potentially catastrophic range of atmospheric, climatic, and radiological consequences of a major nuclear exchange involving 5000 or more megatonnes. Large changes in the optical depth of the atmosphere would occur. Optical depth is a dimensionless quantity determined by particles in the atmosphere (the smoke and dust raised by an explosion) which, due to absorption and scattering, would interrupt a beam of light shining directly down. It is thus a measure of the opacity of a column of atmosphere. The dust, which is injected into the stratosphere, has a longer-lasting effect than the smoke, which is confined to the troposphere whence it is washed out within a month or two. Optical-depth simulations (Fig. 4.5a) show that a range of exchanges between 3000 and 10 000 Mt (Cases 1, 2, 9, and 10) create similar effects. Even Cases 11, 12, and 13, though less severe in their absolute impacts, generate optical depths comparable to, or greater than, those associated with a major volcanic explosion. The calculated optical depths for the El Chichón volcanic eruption cloud are given in Fig. 4.5a. Case 14 represents a 100-Mt attack on cities with 100-kt warheads. About 100 major

TABLE 4.2. *Nuclear-exchange scenarios*

Case	Total yield (Mt)	Surface bursts (% of yield)	Urban or industrial targets (% of yield)	Warhead yield range (Mt)	Total no. of explosions
1. Baseline exchange[a]	5 000	57	20	0.1–10	10 400
2. Low-yield airbursts	5 000	10	33	0.1–1	22 500
4. Baseline, dust only[b]	5 000	57	20	0.1–10	10 400
9. 10 000 Mt full exchange[c]	10 000	63	15	0.1–10	16 160
10. 3000 Mt exchange	3 000	50	25	0.3–5	5 433
11. 3000 Mt counterforce[d]	3 000	70	0	1–10	2 150
12. 1000 Mt exchange[e]	1 000	50	25	0.2–1	2 250
13. 300 Mt southern hemisphere[f]	300	0	25	1	300
14. 100 Mt city attack[g]	100	0	100	0.1	1 000
16. 5000 Mt silos, 'severe' case[h]	5 000	100	0	5–10	700
17. 10 000 Mt 'severe' case	10 000	63	15	0.1–10	16 160

[a] 12 000 km^2 of inner cities are burned; on every cm^2 an average of 10 g of combustibles are burned, and 1.1% of the burned material rises as smoke. Also, 230 000 km^2 of suburban areas burn, with 1.5 g consumed at each cm^2 and 3.6% rising as smoke.

[b] The same as the baseline case but with no fires.

[c] Although these larger total yields might imply involvement of the entire globe in the war, for ease of comparison hemispherically averaged results are still considered.

[d] A highly conservative case in which it is assumed that no smoke emission occurs, that not a blade of grass is burnt, and that just 25 000 tons of fine dust is raised into the upper atmosphere for every megatonne exploded.

[e] Nominal area of wildfires is reduced from 5×10^5 to 5×10^4 km^2.

[f] Nominal area of wildfires is reduced from 5×10^5 to 5×10^3 km^2.

[g] In contrast to the baseline case, only inner cities burn, but with 20 g/cm^2 consumed (twice that of the baseline case) and the net fire smoke emission is 0.026 g per gram of material burned rising as smoke into the high troposphere. Negligible contribution to the opacity from dust and wildfires.

[h] Same assumptions as for case 11, but with 150 000 tons of fine dust raised into the upper atmosphere per megatonne exploded.

Note: Except where noted, attacks are concentrated in the northern hemisphere.

After Turco *et al.* (1983); Ehrlich *et al.* (1984).

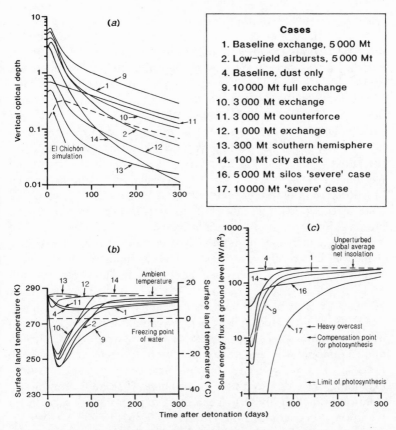

Note: Details of the cases are given in Table 4.2. All variables are averaged over the northern hemisphere. (*a*) Vertical optical depth (scattering plus absorption) of nuclear dust and smoke clouds. Optical depths less than, or equal to, 0.1 have negligible effects; optical depths of around 1 have significant effects, reducing the direct beam radiation to around 37% of its original value; optical depths greater than 2 have major effects. The calculated optical depth for the expanding cloud from the eruption of El Chichón is shown for comparison. (*b*) Surface temperatures. The temperatures generally apply to interior continental land masses. Only in Cases 4 and 11 are the effects of fire neglected. (*c*) Solar energy flux at the ground (insolation). Only in Cases 4 and 16 are fires neglected. Also indicated are the approximate solar flux level at which photosynthesis can only just keep pace with metabolic demands of the plant (respiration)—this is known as the compensation point, and the level at which photosynthesis stops. These levels vary from species to species.

After Ehrlich *et al.* (1984).

F IG. 4.5. Changes in three critical variables in the aftermath of a nuclear war according to various scenarios

cities are assumed to burn. There is negligible contribution to opacity of the atmosphere from dust and wildfires, and most of the urban combustible material is injected into the troposphere, not the stratosphere. This is why the optical depth for this case, though initially high, recovers more swiftly than the baseline case. The simulations suggest a smoke injection threshold for major optical perturbations of about 100 000 000 t. The predicted surface temperature changes over continental land in the northern hemisphere, computed from dust and smoke optical depths, are presented in Fig. 4.5b. The extremely low temperatures occurring within a few weeks of a major exchange are striking. In the baseline case, a minimum land temperature of −23 °C is recorded after three weeks, and sub-freezing temperatures last for several months. Even the most conservative cases (4, 11, and 12) give temperature decreases on land of between about 5 and 10 °C. The reduction in the amount of solar energy reaching the ground owing to the dust and smoke is shown in Fig. 4.5c. For the baseline case, the solar flux at the ground is reduced to less than 10 per cent of its normal value for several weeks.

Taken together, the optical depth, temperature, and insolation effects of major exchanges involve several months of what would almost amount to perpetual night with sub-zero temperatures, even in regions well beyond the targeted zone, and possibly extending into the southern hemisphere. The reduction in insolation is enough in most of the cases to impair plant growth, so disrupting food chains, and in Case 17 (the 10 000-Mt 'severe' case), average light levels fall below the minimum required for photosynthesis for about forty days over much of the northern hemisphere. Even in some of the more moderate exchange scenarios, plants will still struggle to survive as light levels drop below that point at which photosynthesis is just sufficient to maintain plant metabolism, and stay low for around two months. The conclusions drawn from the simulations, not all which are described above, are as follows:

1. Global nuclear war could have a major impact on climate. Significant darkening would last for many weeks, sub-freezing temperatures would persist for up to several months, global circulation patterns would be disrupted, and there would be dramatic changes in local weather and precipitation rates—in

whatever season the exchange took place, a harsh 'nuclear winter', a term coined by Richard Turco, would result. The likelihood that an ice age would be precipitated is very small.

2. Relatively small nuclear exchanges (100–1000 Mt) could produce fairly large climatic effects if urban areas were heavily targeted. This result is unexpected, and means that even limited nuclear exchanges could have severe climatic repercussions.

3. Sooty smoke released by fires ignited by nuclear airbursts would probably have a greater climatic impact than the dust raised by surface bursts, when both occur. This is because smoke particles are very small, with radii of less than 1 μm, and have relatively long atmospheric residence times. All nuclear exchanges, even those where missile silos are the chief target, are likely to spark widespread fires in cities, forests, and grasslands.

4. Smoke from urban areas may perturb climate more than smoke from collateral forest fires, because cities storing large amounts of combustible material are sure to be prime targets, and because the intense firestorms which would rage in cities could pump smoke into the stratosphere, where the residence time is a year or more. Forest fires would loft smoke into the troposphere, but not the stratosphere.

5. Nuclear dust may have a climatic impact, though the effect depends very much on how the war is waged. The effect will be least when lower-yield weapons are deployed and airbursts dominate landbursts.

6. Exposure to radioactive fallout may be more intense and more widespread than predicted by empirical exposure models, which neglect intermediate fallout extending over many days and weeks.

7. The combined effects of a nuclear exchange could place severe stress on the biosphere: the first-order effects predicted by the models involve the disruption of global climates and have even graver consequences than was originally imagined.

The results of this study have been explained in some detail because they have become classic, and have been widely discussed. However, they were the product of the first generation of climate models used to probe the climatic impacts of a nuclear war. Three later generations of models made different assumptions about the processes involved, and led to a somewhat different set of conclusions. We shall discuss the results of the second-, third-, and fourth-generation models because they illustrate how the process of mathematical modelling works in practice: a set of assumptions about a system are made; a model is set up; predictions are made. Later, the assumptions about the system are changed, or the structure of the model is modified (one would hope improved), and revised predictions made. The process continues, adjustments being made to accommodate new empirical findings and theoretical ideas.

Revised Predictions: Prolonged Cold Spells

Whereas the first-generation modellers of the effects of a nuclear exchange used a one-dimensional radiative-convective climate model, the second-generation modellers employed more realistic, three-dimensional atmospheric general circulation models. They assumed a fixed vertical and latitudinal distribution of smoke, and either ignored, or treated by assuming a rate of removal independent of the perturbed climate, the transport and removal of smoke. Their purpose was, initially at least, to explore the moderating effect of the oceans on land-surface temperatures in the post-war period. One research group, comprising Curt Covey, Stephen H. Schneider, and Starley L. Thompson, all of the National Center for Atmospheric Research, Boulder, Colorado, found that enough smoke to give a visible absorption optical depth of 3 (roughly 180 Tg) over the latitude band 30–70°N caused, after about 10–20 days, temperatures to decrease in the latitude band by an average of 25 °C in July, about 15 °C in April, and less than 5 °C in January. The April case, which may be compared to the annually averaged solar forcing in one-dimensional models, suggests that the moderating influence of the oceans roughly halved the temperature drop (Covey *et al.*, 1985). Several other significant findings were made using the second-generation models, all of which indicated that simulations with even more physically realistic assumptions were called for. The findings were (Schneider and Thompson, 1988): a distortion of the atmospheric circulation severe enough in spring and summer to carry smoke into the stratosphere and southern latitudes; a probable change in global precipitation patterns, especially the monsoon rains; and a very non-uniform response of land-surface and sea-surface temperatures, even under a uniformly thick cloud

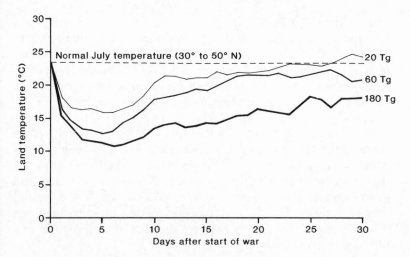

Source: Schneider and Thompson (1988: fig. 2). (Copyright © 1988 Macmillan Magazines Limited. Reprinted by permission.)

FIG. 4.6. Mid-latitude average land-surface temperatures for July GCM simulations with three initial smoke amounts as indicated

of smoke. Other work, which revealed that the air a few metres above the ground could be several degrees warmer than the land surface, pointed to a need to improve the modelling of near-surface atmospheric processes. And it was recognized that the radiation models should incorporate the ability of the smoke to scatter sunlight, and its opacity to infra-red radiation.

The third-generation modellers addressed these research topics and tried to make good the deficiencies of the earlier models. They improved the radiative transfer calculations, and allowed for interactive transport and removal of smoke by smoke-perturbed circulation systems and by precipitation. Attention was focused on the so-called 'acute effects' of a nuclear war: the climatic changes occurring within the first month or two following the injection of smoke into the atmosphere. The team working at the National Center for Atmospheric Research, for example, investigated the sensitivity of average land-surface temperatures to three levels of smoke injections: 20 Tg, 60 Tg, and 180 Tg (Fig. 4.6). The 180-Tg baseline case is equivalent to an injection of 50 Tg of carbon soot, the 60-Tg case to about 16.6 Tg of carbon soot, and the 20-Tg case to about 5.5 Tg of carbon soot. The baseline July case has a maximum average land-surface temperature drop in mid-latitudes of about 10 °C below normal. This is about half the cooling found in the second-generation models with static smoke, and arises largely from two processes: the infra-red opacity of the smoke creating some greenhouse warming, and the patchiness of the smoke distribution allowing solar heating when skies are fairly clear. There is no doubt that the third-generation models fail to produce the extreme falls of surface temperature over land areas which were sustained by the first-generation models, and so dispel the image of a planet frozen for several months. But they still generate rapid cooling episodes with transient, quick freezes, and suggest serious climatic perturbations lasting months and even years. By no means do they brighten the harrowing prospects of a full-scale nuclear exchange.

Chronic Climatic Effects

All three-dimensional models exhibit a patchy land-surface temperature response, resulting from the patchy distribution of the smoke cloud (Fig. 4.7). Substantial surface cooling can occur under the cloud patches, even to below freezing point in July under suitable meteorological conditions (Fig. 4.8). The question of so-called 'chronic' atmospheric effects, that is, effects taking place about a month after the war, would arise from the smoke in the atmosphere which had not been removed by precipitation. The amount of remnant smoke would depend very much on the nuclear-exchange scenario: small smoke injections during winter wars would largely be scavenged within a month of the exchange, whereas smoke from mainly urban targets hit during the summer would keep the smoke levels boosted for several months. To study long-term effects requires the use of coupled atmosphere–ocean GCMs, since sea-surface temperature changes and sea-ice forma-

Note: (*a*) Initial temperatures (before the smoke injection) on day 0. (*b*) Temperatures on day 5. (*c*) Temperatures on day 10. (*d*) Temperatures on day 20.

Source: Schneider and Thompson (1988: fig. 3). (Copyright © 1988 Macmillan Magazines Limited. Reprinted by permission.)

FIG. 4.7. Land-surface temperatures from a July GCM simulation in which 180 Tg of smoke was injected over NATO and Warsaw Pact areas over the first two days

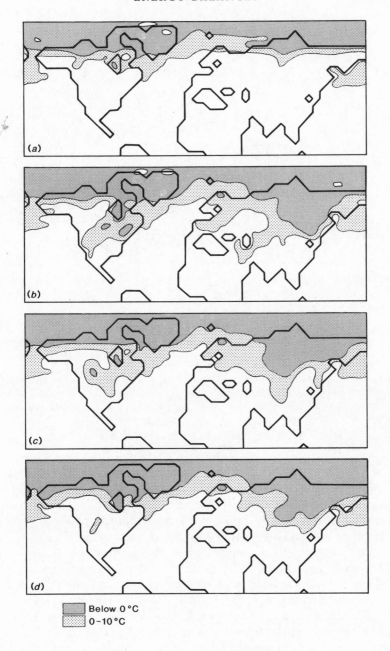

Below 0 °C
0–10 °C

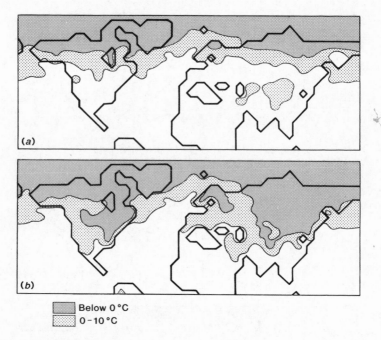

Below 0 °C
0 - 10 °C

Note: (*a*) Unperturbed control case. (*b*) Perturbed case in which 180 Tg of smoke was injected over NATO and Warsaw Pact areas over the first two days.

Source: Schneider and Thompson (1988: fig. 5). (Copyright © 1988 Macmillan Magazines Limited. Reprinted by permission.)

FIG. 4.8. The coldest land-surface temperatures reached at any time during 30-day July simulations

tion need to be included in considerations of climatic changes taking place over several months. Such fourth-generation models suggest that chronic effects are significant. Processes leading to chronic effects include absorption at high altitudes of some 5–40 per cent of incoming solar energy for at least a year. This would reduce surface heating and promote the occurrence of late spring and early autumn frosts. It could also, by narrowing the differences between land and sea temperatures in summer months, lead to a strong reduction in the Asian and African monsoon rains.

So, although many of the world's population would probably survive the initial effects of a nuclear war, they would have to contend with the potential agricultural disasters which would follow in the wake of long-term climatic changes. These, and other, long-term effects on the environment are discussed in the volume edited by Mark A. Harwell and Thomas C. Hutchinson (1985). The prognostications make grim reading: the initial nuclear strikes and their direct effects would probably kill several hundred million people; the indirect effects, which include radical changes in agricultural productivity and food availability, could kill one to several billion people. The loss of all humans is unlikely. Fortunately, the spectre of a nuclear Armageddon has faded with the demise of the Soviet Union. This does not mean that the efforts of the scientists working on the nuclear-war simulations were made in vain: they have aided rapid progress on several research fronts (Schneider, 1988): assessing the chemical and dynamical properties of fires; studying optical properties of smoke; the development and use of interactive chemical, dynamical, radiative, three-dimensional GCMs; and studies of the vulnerability of social and ecological systems to rapid climatic disruption. And the knowledge and models derived from nuclear-war simulations may be applied to other situations where the climate system is suddenly forced by external factors—forcing by volcanic eruptions and by asteroidal impacts are cases in point.

Burning Oil Wells in Kuwait

Nuclear wars have, mercifully, been waged only in computers. Conventional wars *have* taken place. Although they can involve precision bombing, surgical strikes, and the like, where the impact on the environment is kept to a minimum, they have also involved carpet bombing and the use of defoliants, as in Vietnam, and the wilful burning of oil wells, as in Kuwait.

The possible environmental effects of the burning of oil wells in Kuwait were subjected to investigation using various atmospheric models. In one set of experiments, four models were used in tandem (Browning *et al.*, 1991). First, a simple plume model was used to predict the initial behaviour of the plume of oxides of carbon, sulphur, and nitrogen, and unburnt hydrocarbon particulates (soot). A medium-scale weather-prediction model was then employed to simulate the additional increase in height owing to solar heating, the plume shape, and the daytime reduction in surface temperature within a few hundred kilometres of Kuwait.

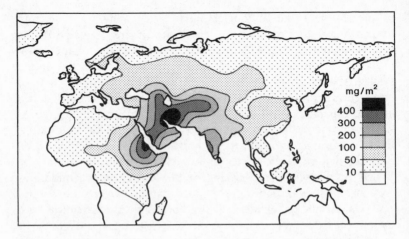

Note: The results are for the worst-case scenario in which 440 000 tonnes of oil (roughly 3.1 million barrels) are burnt per day.

After Bakan *et al.* (1991).

FIG. 4.9. The total deposition of soot (mg/m^2) predicted by the 12-month simulation of the burning oil wells of Kuwait

Thirdly, a long-range dispersion model was used to predict the fate of the plume and to estimate rates of wet and dry deposition. Lastly, data from a trajectory model were used as a basis for GCM integrations to determine the effect of the plume on the Asian summer monsoon. The simulations indicated that most of the smoke from the oil fires would remain in the lowest few kilometres of the troposphere; that, beneath the plume, there would be a severe reduction in daylight, and a daytime temperature drop of about 10 °C within some 200 km of the source; that there would be episodic occurrences of acid rain and photochemical smog up to 2000 km from Kuwait; but that the changes induced in the Asian summer monsoon were unlikely to exceed the changes associated with the natural, year-to-year monsoonal variability.

The possible response of the global climate system to the oil fires was investigated in a series of numerical experiments using a coupled atmosphere–ocean GCM with an interactive soot-transport model and extended radiation scheme (Bakan *et al.*, 1991). Soot released by the fires, even in the worst-case scenario, resides in the atmosphere for relatively short periods of time: the residence time of soot in the troposphere is about 20 days. Most of the soot is washed out of the air by rain and deposited on the ground or at sea within a few thousand kilometres of the source (Fig. 4.9). The maximum deposition—400 mg/m^2—after a year of continual burning occurs in Iran. The climatic response to the soot injections was predicted to be as follows: a 4 °C reduction in surface air temperature in the Gulf region; small and statistically insignificant changes beyond the Gulf region; and no weakening of the Asian summer monsoon. All these predictions are in line with the prognoses made by Browning and his colleagues (1991) in their study.

5

Biogeochemical Cycles

There is in the biosphere a constant turnover of chemicals. The motive force behind these chemical cycles is life. In addition, on geological time-scales, the cycles are influenced by forces in the geosphere producing and consuming rocks. Biogeochemical cycles, as they are called, involve the storage and flux of all terrestrial elements and compounds except the inert ones. Whilst it is true that the nature of biogeochemical cycles is ever-changing, with concomitant alterations in the state of the systems of the biosphere (atmospheric composition, for instance), there is substantial evidence that the storage and, even more so, the flux of many biogeochemicals, including carbon, sulphur, and phosphorus, are being drastically changed by human activities. The consequences of these human perturbations of the biogeochemical system over geological time are unclear, though some simulations suggest long-delayed, radical shifts in the state of the biosphere. Of more immediate concern are changes in the next century. A huge amount of time and effort has gone into studying the potential changes in the global carbon cycle created by the increased flux of carbon dioxide to the atmosphere and its accumulation there. We have already seen how this build-up of carbon dioxide in the air is causing readings on the global thermometer to increase. In this chapter, we shall explore two models, one distributional and one spatial, which set greenhouse-gas-induced climatic change in the context of the world carbon cycle. Emphasis in these models is on the changing stores and fluxes of carbon brought about by human actions.

A Model to Assess the Greenhouse Effect

A prime example of a distributional model, built to simulate the effects of increasing greenhouse-gas concentrations on the biosphere, goes by the acronym IMAGE (Integrated Model to

Assess the Greenhouse Effect) (Rotmans, 1990). It tries to capture the basic aspects of climatic change in a simplified way, but is much broader in scope than the IPCC model mentioned in the previous chapter. It is a multidisciplinary model, involving economics, atmospheric chemistry, marine and terrestrial bio-geochemistry, ecology, climatology, and glaciology. The full model comprises a set of models, called modules by Jan Rotmans, each of which functions, in large measure, independently. None the less, the models are interconnected: the state variables of one influence the state variables of others. In practice, this means that the output of one model is the input to another model further down the causal chain. The key models are a world energy model, a spreadsheet model for other sources of greenhouse gases, an emissions model, an atmospheric-chemistry model, a carbon cycle model, a climate model, and a sea-level-rise model (Fig. 5.1).

The entire model represents a dynamical system within which the effects of greenhouse gases are considered. Formulated in mathematical terms, the model consists of a large set of ordinary, first-order differential equations. Time is considered as discrete steps of six months, and each simulation run covers 200 years of actual time, starting in 1900, roughly corresponding to the close of the pre-industrial era, and ending in 2100. The equations are solved using the Runge–Kutta algorithm for numerical integration, or, in some runs, a more sophisticated method. A brief explanation of each model will now follow.

Emissions Model

This model includes the trace gases carbon dioxide, methane, carbon monoxide, nitrous oxide, CFC-11, CFC-12, and CFC-113. Annual estimates of historical emissions and current emissions are fed into the model for the period 1900–85. For the period 1985–2100, four scenarios were set up. These are very similar to the scenarios mentioned in the context of greenhouse warming discussed earlier.

In summary, Scenario A assumes unrestricted trends with a major increase of energy consumption based on fossil fuels (coal), no incentives to increase the efficiency of energy use, an increasing per capita energy use (especially in the Third World), no stimulation in the use of renewable and non-fossil energy, economic growth not curtailed by environmental considerations, and a rapid

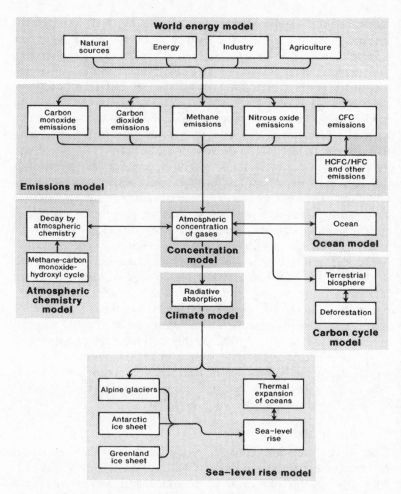

FIG. 5.1. General structure of the IMAGE model

conversion of available forest resources by shifting cultivation, by the demand for wood as a fuel and timber, and for grazing land. Scenario B assumes reduced trends: price increases due to resources becoming scarcer and the imposition of some costs for environmental damage: consequently, there is a slight shift towards non-fossil-fuel energy sources, a minor increase in per capita energy consumption, increasing energy efficiency, and a gradual reduction in the rates of deforestation. Scenario C assumes changing trends: concern over the condition of the environment leads to modest changes in policy: there are incentives for an increased efficiency of energy use and for shifts towards renewable energy sources; and efforts are made across the globe to reduce the rates of deforestation. Scenario D assumes forced trends: major policy changes are implemented owing to grave concern over the prospect of greenhouse warming: there is a reduction in the use of fossil fuels, a vigorous effort to promote greater energy efficiency, a stagnation of the world economy, and a strenuous effort to halt deforestation by forest management and reforestation programmes. The historical and future emissions under the four scenarios are shown in Fig. 5.2.

Concentration Model

The emissions model for trace gases provides the input to the concentration model. Trace gas emissions are linked to an atmospheric-chemistry model, trace-gas storage equations being expressed as:

$$\frac{d\mathrm{p}X}{dt} = \left(\begin{array}{l}\text{conversion factor}\\\text{for trace gas } X\end{array}\right)\left(\begin{array}{l}\text{global emission}\\\text{of trace gas } X\end{array}\right)$$
$$- \left(\begin{array}{l}\text{removal rate}\\\text{of trace gas } X\end{array}\right)\left(\begin{array}{l}\text{tropospheric concentration}\\\text{of trace gas } X\end{array}\right)$$

where $d\mathrm{p}X/dt$ is time rate of change of the concentration of trace gas X in the troposphere. The fluxes are measured in Tg/yr, and the rate constants are expressed as per year. In addition, the emission and concentration of carbon dioxide is linked to an ocean model and to a deforestation model, the latter being integrated into the biospherical component of a carbon cycle model. The historical and predicted concentrations of atmospheric gases for the four scenarios are shown in Fig. 5.3.

Climate Model

Climate is simulated using a radiative-convective model. The computed trace-gas concentrations drive the climate model. Basically, the total change in radiative forcing is the cumulative

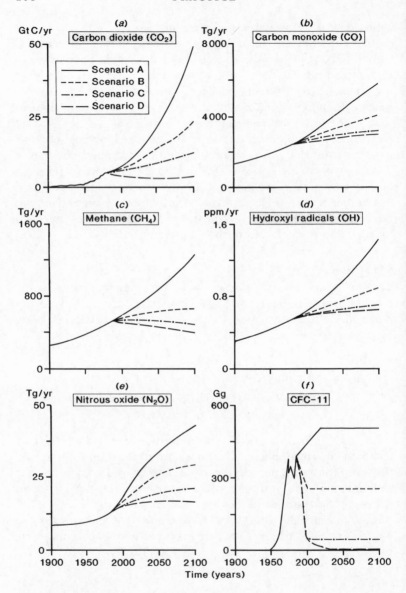

After Rotmans (1990: figs. 4.4, 4.5, 4.6, 4.7, 5.2, 6.3).

FIG. 5.2. Historical and predicted emissions of carbon dioxide, carbon monoxide, methane, and nitrous oxide, and historical and predicted production of hydroxyl radicals and CFC-11, according to the IMAGE model

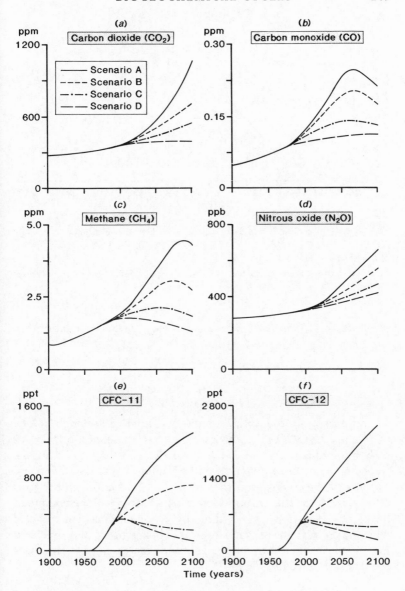

Note: The values for methane are global tropospheric averages.

After Rotmans (1990: figs. 3.8, 4.8, 4.9, 5.3, 6.6, 6.7).

FIG. 5.3. Historical and predicted concentrations of carbon dioxide, carbon monoxide, methane, and nitrous oxide, hydroxyl radicals, and CFC-11, according to the IMAGE model

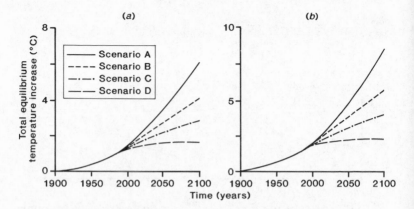

Note: (*a*) Assumes a global carbon dioxide doubling equilibrium temperature of 2.25 °C. (*b*) Assumes a global carbon dioxide doubling equilibrium temperature of 3.0 °C.

After Rotmans (1990: figs. 7.2, 7.3).

FIG. 5.4. Historical and predicted global mean equilibrium temperature increases according to the IMAGE model

effect of the forcings of individual trace gases. The relationship employed is:

$$\Delta Q_{total} = 6.23 \cdot ln(pCO_2/pCO_2in) + 0.0398(\sqrt{pCH_4}$$
$$- \sqrt{pCH_4in}) + 0.105(\sqrt{pN_2O} - \sqrt{pN_2Oin})$$
$$+ 0.27pCFC\text{-}11 - 0.31pCFC\text{-}12$$

where ΔQ_{total} is the total change in radiative forcing; pCO_2, pCH_4, pN_2O, $pCFC\text{-}11$, and $pCFC\text{-}12$ are the concentrations of carbon dioxide, methane, nitrous oxide, CFC-11, and CFC-12 respectively; pCO_2in, pCH_4in, and pN_2Oin are the initial concentrations of the trace gases, that is, the concentrations in the year 1900. The mean equilibrium surface temperature can be computed using this equation by dividing by a climatic-feedback factor which takes account of water vapour. The historical and predicted global mean equilibrium temperature increases for the four scenarios are given in Fig. 5.4.

Sea-Level-Rise Model

One of the most hazardous results of global warming will be the rise of sea level. Nigh on a third of the world's population lives within 60 km of a coastline. A rise of just 1 m would force millions of people to migrate. It is crucial, therefore, to predict as confidently as possible the likely sea-level rise associated with various emission scenarios. Modelling sea-level change induced by global warming is no easy task. It is hampered by shortcomings in our knowledge of the processes involved. Except in environments where subsidence is significant, three factors appear to determine sea-level change over a time-scale of decades and centuries: the thermal expansion of sea water, the melting of valley glaciers, and the reaction of land ice. These factors are undoubtedly being influenced by human activities, but they also change in response to natural climatic variability. Teasing out the human influence from the background of natural variation is a tricky feat.

Thermal expansion is believed to be the single most important contributor to sea-level rise. It has been modelled using a simple energy-balance box-diffusion model of the climate system. This model includes a land store, an ocean store, and two atmosphere stores—one over land and one over oceans. The storage equation in the energy-balance model may be written

$$C_m \frac{d\Delta T}{dt} = \Delta Q - \lambda \Delta T - \Delta F$$

where C_m is the bulk heat capacity of the ocean mixed layer, ΔT is the change in temperature of the ocean mixed layer, ΔQ is the perturbation in the energy flux to the surface, λ is a climate sensitivity parameter and represents a change in climate due to a given radiative forcing, ΔQ, and ΔF is a change in the heat flux at the bottom of the mixed layer.

The temperature changes calculated by the climate model in the IMAGE model drive the sea-level-rise model. Five processes are taken into account in this model: the thermal expansion of ocean water, the melting of alpine glaciers, the ablation of the Greenland ice sheet, the accumulation of ice on Antarctica, and a natural trend in sea-level change. The model uses a single ocean column divided into a mixed ocean layer 75 m thick, and 37 deep ocean layers, each 25 m thick. It considers climatic perturbations (global warming), the extra heat being allowed to diffuse through the ocean layers. Each layer is given its own thermal expansion coefficient and thus each makes its own contribution to thermal expansion. Integrating contributions over the simulation period then yields the total sea-level rise by thermal expansion. Rotmans (1990) also included in his model the effects of glaciers and small ice-sheets, the Greenland ice-sheet, and the Antarctic ice-sheet.

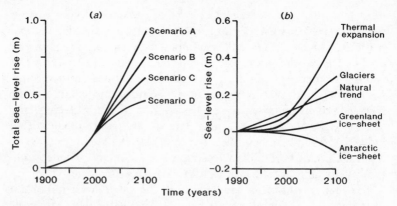

Note: (*a*) Total sea-level rise for different scenarios. (*b*) Components of sea-level rise for Scenario A (unrestricted trends).

Source: Rotmans (1990: figs. 8.1, 8.2).

FIG. 5.5. Historical and predicted changes of sea level according to the IMAGE model

Although the Greenland and Antarctic ice-sheets might seem to dwarf the smaller ice-sheets and glaciers, the latter actually contain enough water to raise sea level by 33 cm. It is possible that greenhouse warming accounts for half the glacier retreat over the last century, the other half being attributable to volcanic activity. If fully melted, the water stored in the Greenland ice-sheet would raise sea level by about 7.5 m, and the water stored in the Antarctic ice-sheet would raise sea level by about 65 m.

The big problem with sea-level-rise projections is the uncertainties in the various contributions of individual ice-sheets and glaciers. Bearing this problem in mind, Rotmans (1990) predicted sea-level rise to the year 2100 under four scenarios. The rise varies from 0.95 m under Scenario A to 0.45 m under Scenario D (Fig. 5.5*a*). The individual contribution of the components of sea-level change in Scenario A are depicted in Fig. 5.5*b*. Plainly, thermal expansion is the chief contributor, with glaciers coming second. The melting of the Greenland ice and the accumulation of ice on Antarctica have a small effect on the results. Thermal expansion and glacier melting are projected to play a relatively more important role over the next century. Rotmans's projected figures are in fair agreement with rates quoted in the literature, though they may be fractionally high because the upwelling of ocean water was not included in his model.

Carbon-Cycle Model

This consists of several interrelated models: an emission model, an atmospheric-concentration model, an ocean model, a terrestrial-biosphere model, and a deforestation model. The carbon dioxide emission model generates input for the atmospheric model. Both these models are linked to the ocean and terrestrial models. Three anthropogenic sources of carbon dioxide are included in the emission model: fossil-fuel combustion, the production of cement, and land-use changes. The last of these is incorporated in the deforestation model. The historical and projected emissions of carbon dioxide are displayed in Fig. 5.2. Of key importance to the understanding of greenhouse warming is the airborne fraction of carbon dioxide. This is defined in the model as

$$\text{Airborne fraction of } CO_2 = \frac{\text{net increase of carbon dioxide in the atmosphere}}{\text{fossil fuel emission} - \text{net uptake by terrestrial biota}}$$

$$= \frac{\dfrac{\text{fossil fuel}}{\text{emission}} - \dfrac{\text{uptake}}{\text{by ocean}} + \dfrac{\text{net uptake by}}{\text{terrestrial biota}}}{\text{fossil fuel emission} - \text{net uptake by terrestrial biota}}$$

where

$$\begin{array}{l}\text{net uptake by} \\ \text{terrestrial} \\ \text{biota}\end{array} = \begin{array}{l}\text{emission from} \\ \text{terrestrial biota by} \\ \text{human disturbance}\end{array} - \begin{array}{l}\text{uptake by} \\ \text{terrestrial} \\ \text{biota}\end{array}$$

The airborne fraction of carbon dioxide is the main product of the carbon-cycle model. Simulated results are shown in Fig. 5.6 for the four scenarios, along with historical information. In Scenario D, the airborne fraction of carbon dioxide decreases to about 25 per cent by the year 2100. This is because, under the assumptions of this scenario, the uptake of carbon dioxide by oceans and the terrestrial biota roughly balances the release of carbon dioxide by the burning of fossil fuels and changes of land use. In Scenario A, it rises to about 75 per cent at that date.

The atmosphere is treated as a well-mixed store of carbon dioxide, with a mixing time of one year. Changes in atmospheric

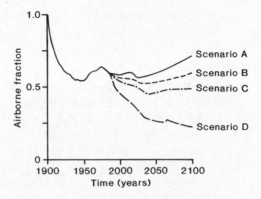

Note: The airborne fraction of carbon dioxide is defined as the fraction of carbon dioxide emissions from fossil fuel and changes in the biosphere which remains in the atmosphere

Source: Rotmans (1990: fig. 3.7).

FIG. 5.6. Historical and predicted values of the airborne fraction of carbon dioxide according to the IMAGE model

carbon dioxide levels are modelled by the following storage equation:

$$\frac{d\mathrm{pCO_2}}{dt} = 0.471 \begin{pmatrix} \text{fossil fuel emissions} \\ + \text{flux from ocean to atmosphere} \\ - \text{net ecosystem production} \\ + \text{flux due to human activity} \end{pmatrix}$$

where $d\mathrm{pCO_2}/dt$ is the time rate of change of carbon dioxide stored in the atmosphere (Gt C/yr), and the constant 0.471 converts stores of carbon measured in gigatonnes to parts per million by volume (ppmv). Carbon dioxide concentrations under the four scenarios are shown in Fig. 5.3.

Carbon in the oceans is modelled by a one-dimensional box-diffusion model in which the ocean is represented as twelve layers. The two surface layers are a warm mixed layer 75 m deep, and a cold mixed layer 400 m deep. There is one intermediate layer, 1005 m deep, and nine layers each 680 m deep. The carbon concentration in the ocean is determined by three processes in the model: carbon transport by the mass flow of water, i.e. by ocean currents; carbon movement by turbulent mixing (diffusion); and carbon movement by the precipitation of carbon compounds.

Further details of this model may be found in Rotmans (1990: 35–40).

The terrestrial-biosphere model is an extended version of the model devised by Jan Goudriaan and P. Ketner (1984) and described earlier in the book. Basically, it divides the terrestrial biosphere into seven stores—leaves, branches, stems, roots, litter, humus, and stable humus charcoal. The effect of deforestation on these stores is added through a separate, detailed deforestation model. The driving force of the model is net primary production, and the effect of carbon dioxide fertilization on primary production is included. The deforestation model is an independent submodel of the carbon-cycle model. Its structure is laid out in Fig. 5.7. In brief, it recognizes four ecosystems where deforestation, and concomitant land-use change, are significant: tropical forests, grasslands, arable land, and semi-desert. Tropical forests are subdivided into open and closed canopy forests. All converted forests are assumed to end up as re-established forests, agricultural or pasture land, or degraded areas. Deforestation is induced by several processes, all of which are chiefly the result of demographic and economic pressures. The transitions from one type of land use to another are described by differential equations. For instance, the amount of closed tropical forest is determined by the initial amount of closed tropical forest and its conversion into arable land, pasture, other land, and open tropical forest:

$$\frac{dCF}{dt} = \begin{aligned} &- \text{ logging by commercial wood production} \\ &- \text{ industrial or mining projects} \\ &- \text{ shifting cultivation in closed forest} \\ &- \text{ expansion of arable land into closed forest} \\ &- \text{ expansion of pasture into closed forest} \end{aligned}$$

where dCF/dt is the rate of conversion of tropical closed forest to other land uses. Several of these processes may become negative and the deforestation process become reversed. Further details of this complex model are given by Rotmans (1990: 47–61). Fig. 5.8 gives the flavour of the results obtainable using the deforestation model. Taking Asia as an example, it shows the simulated changes in logging, reforestation by plantations, area of closed tropical forest, area of open tropical forest, area of agricultural land, and the degradation of agricultural land, under the differing assumptions of the four scenarios.

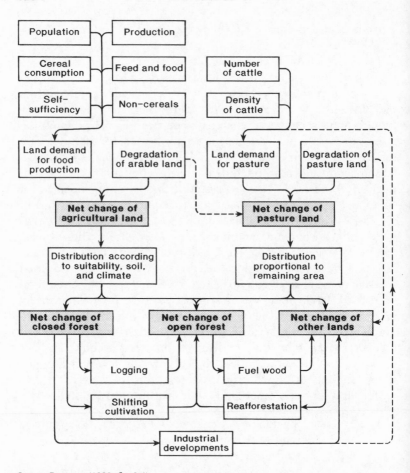

Source: Rotmans (1990: fig. 3.4).

FIG. 5.7. The structure of the IMAGE deforestation model

Global Warming and the IMAGE Model

The chief conclusions from experiments made with the IMAGE model are as follows:

1. If carbon dioxide emissions continue at the present rate, then the atmospheric concentration of carbon dioxide will rise rapidly, doubling its 1985 level by the year 2060. Even when radical measures are adopted to curb emissions (Scenario D), the

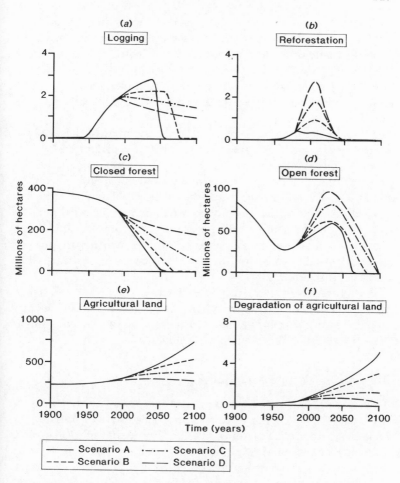

After Rotmans (1990: figs. 3.5, 3.6, 3.9, 3.10, 3.13, 3.14).

FIG. 5.8. Variables predicted by the IMAGE deforestation model for Asia

atmospheric carbon dioxide level will rise, though the time taken to double the 1985 level is postponed to beyond the year 2100.

2. The contribution of changes in carbon storage in the terrestrial biosphere to the greenhouse effect is not insignificant, but nevertheless small in comparison with the contribution made by the burning of fossil fuels.

3. The immediate cause of deforestation is the demand for agricultural land to satisfy the pressing need of many countries for food for home consumption and for products for export to reduce debts.

4. If present rates of deforestation continue unabated, total destruction of tropical forest will occur half-way through the next century.

5. Deforestation, even when it proceeds swiftly, has only a moderate effect on the carbon cycle. The effect is limited because of the ability of the soil carbon pool to 'soak up' organic matter converted to charcoal on burning, and the fertilization of phytomass by atmospheric carbon dioxide. Of course, the less vegetation there is, the less phytomass there is to be fertilized.

6. The deforestation model raises the real promise of building a workable model of global land-use change which can provide practical insights into the interactions between human activities and the biosphere.

7. Reforestation can offset the effects of deforestation, but a change to a world energy system based on renewable energy sources is a far more potent weapon with which to combat greenhouse-gas-induced changes of climate.

The Osnabrück Biosphere Model

This is a spatial model which tries to capture the dynamics of the carbon cycle in the terrestrial biosphere. It was initiated by Helmut Lieth and developed at the University of Osnabrück, Germany, between 1980 and 1990, being presented for the first time at a symposium sponsored by the Commission of the European Communities in March 1983 and held at Osnabrück. The version reported by Gerd Esser, its chief designer, in 1991 uses grid-cells 2.5° × 2.5° (latitude × longitude) in size. With Antarctica excluded, this level of resolution gives 2433 grid-cells. A new version of the model is currently being programmed which will use a higher spatial resolution (0.5° × 0.5°) and a finer time resolution—one month as opposed to one year.

An important departure of the Osnabrück model from other models, such as the IMAGE model, is that primary production is powered by environmental factors (climate, soil, human impacts, and so on), rather than being correlated with vegetation units. The rationale behind this difference in approach is that, of the total 2433 grid-cells, net primary production data has been measured for, at most, a mere 150. In contrast, global climate data sets are available for over 7000 World Meteorological Organization standard stations. Given that ecological fluxes are more strongly correlated with environmental influences than with vegetation units, it seems wise to opt for the available, extensive data sets on climate and other environmental factors in lieu of the patchy records of primary production.

Building the Model

To appreciate how the model works, it is helpful to explore in some detail its construction. All the variables in the model are listed in Table 5.1. The notation in this table is the same as that used by Esser (1991). The model computes the storage and transfer of carbon for each store within a grid-cell using appropriate rate constants and other coefficients. To get a feel for the calculations involved, we shall run through the computational formulae for the various stores.

Net Primary Production. Net primary production of natural vegetation, *NPP*, is calculated from an annually integrated two-dimensional array derived from the empirical Miami equation (which relates net primary production to mean annual temperature and mean annual precipitation) and a soil correction factor, $F(m)$:

$$NPP(j,m) = \left[\min\{NPPT(j,m), NPPPp(j,m)\} \cdot F(m) \cdot \left(\frac{AV(j,m)}{AG(m)} \right) \right. $$
$$ \left. + yield(j,m) \cdot FA(m) \cdot \left(\frac{AA(j,m)}{AG(m)} \right) \right] \cdot FCO_2 $$

where the following two functions are from the Miami model:

$$NPPT(j, m) = \frac{3000}{1 + e^{1.315 - 0.119T(j,m)}}$$

$$NPPPp(j, m) = \frac{3000}{1 - e^{-0.000664P_p(j,m)}}$$

TABLE 5.1. *Alphabetical list of variables used in the Osnabrück biosphere model*[a]

Symbol	Meaning	Units
c	field crop	–
i	plant material (woody, herbaceous), $i = h, w$	–
j	model year AD, $j = 1860, \ldots 2100$	–
m	grid-cell, $m = 1, \ldots 2433$	–
o	soil unit, $o = 1, \ldots O(m)$	–
AA	agricultural area of grid-cell m in model year j	m^2
AG	total area of grid-cell m	m^2
AGE	mean stand age of a vegetation unit	yr
AS	area of soil type o in grid cell m	m^2
AV	area covered by natural vegetation in grid-cell m	m^2
c_1, c_2	parameters determining the slope and turning-point of the clearing function	–
CO_2	carbon dioxide concentration in the atmosphere	ppmv
DIS	annual discharge	mm/yr
DOC	dissolved organic carbon export	g/m^2/yr
f	soil factor of soil type o	–
F	weighted mean of all fs of grid-cell m	–
f_a	conversion factor of yield to NPP	–
FA	weighted mean of all the $fa(c)$s of grid-cell m	–
FCO_2	fertilizing factor of CO_2 on NPP	–
H	factor for sharing NPP into i (herbaceous and woody) compartments	–
j_{TP}	year of the turning-point of the logistic clearing function	–
kd	decay coefficient for litter	/yr
klp	litter production coefficient	/yr
$KORR$	factor to correlate $PART(j)$, $j = 1860, \ldots, 1980$, with $PART(1970)$; O $\leq$ KORR $\leq$ 1.5	–
$ksocp$	soil organic carbon production coefficient	/yr
$ksoc$	soil organic carbon depletion coefficient	/yr
k_T	kd derived from T	/yr
k_{Pp}	kd derived from Pp	/yr
L	litter pool	g/m^2
LD	litter depletion	g/m^2/yr
LP	litter production	g/m^2/yr
NPP	net primary productivity	g/m^2/yr
$NPPT$	NPP derived from T	g/m^2/yr
$NPPPp$	NPP derived from Pp	g/m^2/yr
$PART$	part of grid-cell m under agricultural use	%
P	total above- and below-ground phytomass	g/m^2
$SOCP$	soil organic carbon production	g/m^2/yr
POC	particulate organic carbon export	g/m^2/yr
Pp	average annual precipitation	mm/yr
T	average annual temperature	°C
WL	clearing probability derived from land use in the period 1950 to 1980	–
WP	clearing probability derived from NPP	–
WS	clearing probability derived from soil fertility, F	–
WU	clearing probability derived from land use in surrounding grid-cells	–
$yield$	yield of crops in grid-cell m (weighted mean)	g/m^2/yr

[a] Most of the variables are arrays.

After Esser (1991: table 31.3, pp. 684–5).

The soil correction factor is given as

$$F(m) = \frac{\sum\limits_{o=1}^{O(m)} f(o) \cdot AS(m, o)}{\sum\limits_{o=1}^{O(m)} AS(m, o)}$$

and so is calculated as the weighted mean of the soil factors, $f(o)$, of the soils of a grid-cell, m, according to the areas, $AS(m, o)$, which they occupy. FCO_2 is a correction factor for the influence of atmospheric carbon dioxide concentration on net primary production, and is calculated by a regression function derived from a set of data measured in ecological and physiological experiments:

$$FCO_2 = A \cdot \{1 - e^{-R(CO_2(j)-80)}\}$$

where

$$A = 1 + \frac{F(m)}{4}$$

$$R = -\ln\left(\frac{A - 1}{A}\right) \cdot \frac{1}{240}$$

The cultivated area of a grid-cell, $AA(j, m)$, is computed from its value in 1970 modified by a quotient of population in the year j to 1970:

$$AA(j, m) = AA(1970, m) \cdot \left(\frac{PM(j)}{PM(1970)}\right)^z$$

where z is 0.8 and $PM(j)$ is defined as

$$PM(j) = (7.295 \times 10^8) + \{(3.9371 \times 10^7) \cdot e^{0.025(j-1760)}\}$$

The calculated net primary production is then apportioned between woody and herbaceous growth according to a simple linear sharing factor, $H(i)$, ($i = h$ = herbaceous; $i = w$ = woody):

$$NPP(i) = H(i) \cdot NPP$$

$H(i)$ values were calculated for 31 vegetation formations. The herbaceous factor ranged from 0.20 in mangrove to 1.0 in several formations, including herbaceous tundra.

Litter Production. Litter produced by woody and herbaceous material is assumed proportional to the donor phytomass store:

$$LP(i) = klp(i) \cdot P(i)$$

The rate constants $klp(i)$ were derived from mean stand age of plant material in the vegetation formation under consideration and the phytomass share factors $H(i)$:

$$klp(i) = \frac{H(i)}{0.59181 \cdot AGE(i)^{0.79216}}$$

where $AGE(i)$ is the mean stand age of the potential natural vegetation in a grid-cell (see Esser, 1991: 691 for a full derivation).

Litter Depletion. It was assumed that the amount of litter decomposed per year is proportional to the amount of litter in the litter store:

$$\frac{dL}{dt} = -kL$$

The rate constant k depends on temperature and precipitation, and is different for woody, kw, and herbaceous, kh, litter. For any grid-cell, the rate constant for the decay of herbaceous litter was set as the minimum value of the decay due to temperature, $khT(j, m)$, and the decay rate due to precipitation, $khPp(j, m)$. These rates were determined by the empirical relations determined from a global set of 93 field sites (see Esser, 1991; for additional information, see Esser and Lieth, 1989).

Organic Material in Rivers. The fluxes of dissolved organic carbon, DOC, and suspended organic carbon, POC, in the world's rivers were incorporated in the model by taking the annual river flux in 1970 as $1.0\,\mathrm{Gt\,C/yr}$, and then assuming that the annual freight has increased since then in proportion to the increase in agricultural area (see also Esser and Kohlmaier, 1991).

Land-Use Changes and Deforestation. The direct human influence on vegetation acts upon the variables crop yield, $yield(j, m)$, relative agricultural area, $AA(j, m)/AG(j, m)$, and stand age $AGE(i)$. For the period of simulation, the agricultural area of a grid-cell may increase owing to deforestation or decrease owing to reforestation. The model uses historical data for the years to 1980, and for the years after 1980 it applies various scenarios to obtain the relative agricultural area in each grid-cell. The details of this model are too complicated to be tackled here (see Esser, 1989).

Calibrating the Model

In order to run the model, the global pattern of all driving variables resolved at the 2.5° × 2.5° (latitude × longitude) grid-cell level were needed. The list included mean annual temperature, mean annual precipitation, vegetation formation, soil class, and agricultural crops. The following list of data sources serves to illustrate the difficulties of calibrating a spatial model such as this one.

Climate. Mean annual temperature and mean annual precipitation were derived from the World Meteorological Organization's standard network of climate stations (supplied by the National Center for Atmospheric Research, Boulder, Colorado), a world atlas of climate diagrams, and a data collection based on climatic zone maps. The data were interpolated and corrected for the mean elevation of each grid-cell.

Soils. A soil map of the world was digitized on the spatial grid used in the model. Areas covered by the soil units were rendered as a percentage of grid-cell area. 106 soil units were considered. Associated soils were excluded.

Potential Natural Vegetation. A world vegetation map was digitized in the same way as soils were. The 172 vegetation units included in the map were reduced to 31 formations.

Land Use. Country-related statistical data were culled from an atlas of world agriculture, agricultural production yearbooks, and the results of projects in various agro-ecological zones. These data were distributed on the model grid by the use of information supplied by the Agro-Ecological Zones Project.

Land-Use Changes. A factor array for 121 countries and each year during the period 1860–1980 was drawn up, using published data and an evaluation of 934 Landsat images for the years 1972–1980.

Crop Yields. These were derived from various production yearbooks.

TABLE 5.2. *Changes in the terrestrial carbon cycle by latitudinal zones as predicted by the Osnabrück biosphere model*[a]

Hemisphere	Latitudinal zone (°N and °S)	Phytomass change due to carbon dioxide fertilization (Mt C/yr)	Phytomass change due to carbon dioxide fertilization and land-use change (Mt C/yr)	Net effect of land-use change (Mt C/yr)	Total extra carbon in phytomass, soil, and litter (Mt C/yr)
Northern	70–80	1.1	1.0	−0.1	5.6
	60–70	40.4	34.9	−5.5	64.2
	50–60	80.7	62.6	−18.1	10.6
	40–50	102.5	171.1	68.6	143.9
	30–40	67.5	178.1	110.6	116.9
	20–30	80.5	−113.6	−194.1	−50.8
	10–20	82.3	−95.4	−177.7	−71.5
	0–10	233.9	79.5	−154.4	144.7
Southern	10–0	295.0	180.5	−114.5	215.0
	20–10	147.7	67.5	−80.2	115.4
	30–20	90.5	−102.3	−192.8	−57.3
	40–30	19.4	−20.9	−40.3	−31.0
	50–40	9.3	1.8	−7.5	1.6
	60–50	1.1	0.9	−0.2	1.9
Total source		1251.9	445.7		608.2
Total sink				−806.2	

[a] Negative values represent net losses of carbon from vegetation. The reference year is 1980.

After Esser (1991: table 31.9, p. 700).

Experiments with the Model

The model was used to address key questions about the terrestrial biosphere. How important is carbon dioxide fertilization on a global scale, and how is it distributed globally? How do tropical deforestation and other human influences on vegetation affect the carbon balance in the terrestrial biosphere? Several papers report attempts to tackle these issues (e.g. Esser, 1987; 1991). General conclusions which can be drawn from the Osnabrück simulation studies are discussed below.

It is possible that elevated concentrations of atmospheric carbon dioxide will boost the primary production of vegetation on land. This is the effect known as carbon dioxide fertilization. If large enough, it would counteract, at least in some measure, the release of carbon dioxide from the burning of fossil fuels and forest destruction. Table 5.2 lists the zonal integrals of the fertilization effect on several state variables in the Osnabrück biosphere model. Fertilization of vegetation by carbon dioxide increases net primary production. Assuming that stand age remain unchanged (there is no experimental work supporting or invalidating this assumption), then the phytomass of mature stands will increase and they will become a sink in the global cycle of carbon. The stores of carbon in litter and soil organic matter will also rise. Deforestation counteracts the sink in the phytomass storage (by reducing stand age), and in the litter and soil organic matter stores (by reduced phytomass productivity). Carbon dioxide fertilization and de-forestation work hand in hand. Their individual effects, at global and regional scales, can be unravelled by the model. It can be seen in Table 5.2 (column 1) that carbon dioxide fertilization generates the most extra phytomass in the humid tropics, then in the moist subtropical and temperate forests. The effect in boreal forest regions is very small, owing to the low productivity and phyto-mass in those areas. The zonal sums of extra phytomass created by fertilization are shown in the table for the reference year 1980. It is apparent that, in total, 1251.9 Mt C were sequestered into global phytomass, 758.9 Mt (60 per cent) of it in the latitude zone sandwiched between 20°S and 20°N. The total phytomass change, caused by land-use changes including deforestation, in each latitudinal zone is shown in Table 5.2, column 2. Land-use changes counterbalance the increase of phytomass generated by

TABLE 5.3. *Change in major stores of carbon in the terrestrial biosphere from 1860 to 1980 according to a model with standard climate (no climatic change)*

Year	Atmosphere (ppmv)	Carbon stores				Accumulative fluxes	
		Natural phytomass (Gt C)	Agricultural phytomass (Gt C)	Litter (Gt C)	Soil (Gt C)	Deforestation (Gt C)	Fertilization effect (Gt C)
1860	285.0	668	1.6	91	1536	−0	0
1870	286.7	663	1.7	92	1537	−7	2
1880	288.6	658	1.9	92	1538	−15	5
1890	290.7	654	2.1	92	1539	−22	8
1900	293.1	650	2.2	92	1539	−30	12
1910	296.1	646	2.4	92	1538	−37	15
1920	299.4	643	2.5	92	1538	−44	19
1930	303.2	639	2.6	92	1538	−54	25
1940	307.0	636	2.8	92	1537	−63	31
1950	311.6	633	2.9	92	1536	−73	38
1960	317.6	634	3.0	92	1535	−81	47
1970	326.5	637	3.1	92	1533	−89	58
1980	338.8	644	3.2	92	1531	−96	73

After Esser (1991: table 31.10, p. 702).

the fertilization effect. It is evident that, of the 1251.9 Mt C sequestered by phytomass owing to the fertilization effect, 445.7 Mt C remains after loss due to land-use changes is accounted for. It should be cautioned that some researchers contend that the growth of vegetation is limited by other factors, and that higher levels of carbon dioxide may have a limited fertilizing effect on primary production. Higher carbon dioxide levels should make it possible for plants to use water more efficiently because stomatae partially close in high concentrations of carbon dioxide. The result would be less moisture drawn from the soil and an increase in runoff and river flow (Probst and Tardy, 1987).

By subtracting column 1 from column 2 in Table 5.2, the change in phytomass due to land-use changes can be found (column 3). Notice that in the zone lying between latitudes 30–50°N there is a net fixation of carbon, probably owing to reforestation. The data in column 4 of the table show the extra carbon stored in the terrestrial biosphere when the secondary effects of carbon dioxide fertilization and land-use changes on soil organic matter and litter are included in the computations. Overall, the terrestrial biosphere takes up an extra 608.2 Mt C/yr as a result of those effects. Surprisingly, given that tropical de-forestation was already well under way at the start of the 1980s, the terrestrial biosphere was actually a net sink for atmospheric carbon at that time. This situation arose because the carbon dioxide fertilization effect, in conjunction with reforestation, more than compensated for the carbon losses. However, the biosphere does not always appear to have been a sink for atmospheric carbon. Simulations made using the Osnabrück biosphere model for the period 1860–1980 suggest that, until 1950, the phytomass decreased owing to deforestation, and the fertilization effect was far too small to compensate for anything but a small part of the carbon losses.

Various simulation runs were made using a standard climate (no climatic change), a temperature increase, and no fertilization effect (net primary production not affected by the concentration of carbon dioxide in the atmosphere). The results (Table 5.3) point to the unrealism of ignoring the fertilization effect in models of the terrestrial carbon cycle, and tend to confirm the significant changes in that cycle being caused by human activities.

6

Water Cycles

The human species is advertently and inadvertently causing global and regional changes in the water cycle, and in the associated solute and sediment transport systems. A range of models exist with which to predict the movement of water through terrestrial environmental systems. Catchment models attempt to predict runoff by tracing the fate of water added in precipitation through a series of storage units and subtracting water lost in evaporation and plant uptake. Each soil-storage unit has a water-holding capacity, and storage in excess of that limit is fed into the next lower soil unit in the soil profile by infiltration, or into the next downslope storage unit in the landscape by throughflow. These models are sometimes coupled to models of soil chemistry to predict solute losses in the runoff. The rates of transfer between stores are governed by parameters and functions, the values of which can allow for spatial variations in the physical characteristics of a catchment. Recently, large-scale catchment models have been built to assess the contribution that land areas make to the global water cycle.

This chapter will explore models concerned with three aspects of water and solute cycles: regional catchment models, models which look at the possible connection between forest clearance and rainfall, and models which simulate the acidification of waters in soil, rock, rivers, and lakes.

Water Balance and Fluvial Transport in South America

A catchment model was built by Charles Vörösmarty and his colleagues (1989) to look into the impact of human activities on the basin water cycle at a large scale. The ultimate use of this model is as part of a bigger model of global biogeochemistry. Its immediate use lies in creating high-resolution sets of data for monthly soil moisture, evapotranspiration, runoff, river discharge, and floodplain inundation. This hydrological information can then be used in models of terrestrial primary production, organic-matter decay, riverine nutrient flux, and trace-gas exchanges with the troposphere. Indirectly, therefore, the model should aid the prediction of the consequences on the biosphere of land-use changes brought about by human activity.

The model was developed at the continental scale and, in the example given here, was used to investigate the water balance and fluvial transport in South America. One reason for choosing this continent was that parts of the Amazonian rain forests are suffering increasingly from disruption by human activities. The study would therefore lay down a bench-mark against which the future climatic effects of human disturbances could be gauged. The building of a hydrological model at a continental scale required a thoughtful simplification of existing catchment hydro-logy models. Key points to note in the simplification process were the need to exploit the data sets currently available in point, polygonal, or grid-cell formats, and the need to specify the minimum number of parameters in calibration, so that eventual global coverage would be facilitated. The model is a coupled water-balance and water-transport model involving storage equations and transport laws (Fig. 6.1). It is spatially disaggre-gated, its spatial domain comprising a set of more than 5700 geographically referenced grid-cells, each $0.5° \times 0.5°$ (latitude × longitude) in size, representing South America.

The Water-Balance Model

In essence, the water-balance model transforms spatially complex biogeophysical data on long-term precipitation, temperature, potential evapotranspiration, vegetation, soils, and elevation, into predictions of soil moisture, evapotranspiration, and runoff for each $0.5°$ grid-cell in the simulated region. The biogeophysical data were derived from large-scale maps of each South American country. These maps were used to characterize the vegetation, soil, and climate in each grid-cell.

The transformation of the biophysical data into monthly pre-dictions of runoff relied on a major refinement of the techniques devised by C. Warren Thornthwaite and J. R. Mather (1957) for computing the water balance at the Earth's surface. Soil moisture is calculated from interactions between rainfall, snowmelt re-

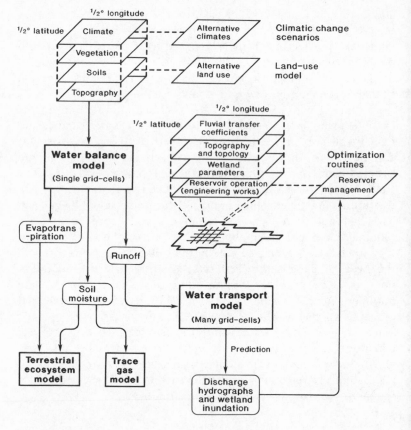

After Vörösmarty *et al.* (1989); Vörösmarty and Moore (1991).

FIG. 6.1. Structure of a global water cycle model, showing the relationships between the water balance model, the water transport model, and a set of gridded data sets

charge, and potential evapotranspiration. During wet months, when rainfall plus snowmelt recharge exceeds potential evapotranspiration, soil moisture is allowed to increase up to a maximum water-holding capacity determined by soil texture and rooting depth. The water-storage equation is, for wet months with initial soil moisture values below field capacity:

$$\frac{dW}{dt} = \text{rainfall} + \text{snowfall} - \text{potential evapotranspiration}$$

where W is soil moisture storage; and for wet months when soil moisture starts at field capacity:

$$\frac{dW}{dt} = 0$$

During dry periods, when rainfall plus snowfall is less than potential evapotranspiration and the soil moisture store is depleted, soil moisture storage is a function of potential water loss according to the following water-storage equation:

$$\frac{dW}{dt} = -aW \,\{\text{potential evapotranspiration} \\ - (\text{rainfall} + \text{snowfall})\}$$

In the water-storage equations, soil moisture is in mm; rainfall, snowfall, and potential evapotranspiration are in mm/month. The parameter a is the slope of the soil moisture retention curve, as described below. Computations start at the end of the wet season, when it is assumed that soil is at field capacity. The store of soil moisture is then depleted during the dry season in accordance with the soil moisture retention curve. As soil dries, so it becomes increasingly difficult to remove soil water against pore tension. The model uses the function

$$a = \frac{\ln(\text{field capacity})}{1.1282(\text{field capacity})^{1.2756}}$$

to define the slope of the soil moisture retention curve. In this expression, the numerator represents soil moisture (mm) with no net drying; the denominator is the accumulated potential water loss (mm), given as the sum of potential evapotranspiration less rainfall plus snowfall, at a soil water storage of 1.0 mm. With a determined, the model computes dW/dt as a function of soil dryness, and then updates W. The soil moisture level is computed to a maximum level set by the field capacity for a particular soil. The degree of waterlogging when this capacity is exceeded is not determined. For each wet month, soil moisture is determined by incrementing antecedent values by the excess of available water over potential evapotranspiration. This recharge of soil water may or may not bring the soil back to field capacity at the close of the subsequent wet season.

After soil moisture levels have been worked out, actual evapotranspiration is calculated according to the following schema.

During wet months, actual evapotranspiration is assumed to equal potential evapotranspiration. During dry seasons, the actual evapotranspiration rate is assumed to fall below the potential rate. The equations used to compute actual evapotranspiration are, for wet seasons, where rainfall plus snowfall exceeds potential evapotranspiration:

actual evapotranspiration = potential evapotranspiration

and for dry seasons, where rainfall plus snowfall is less than potential evapotranspiration:

$$\text{actual evapotranspiration} = \text{rainfall} + \text{snowfall} - \frac{dW}{dt}$$

The next step in the water-balance model is the calculation of runoff. In a grid-cell where field capacity is reached, excess water is routed to subsurface runoff stores for rain and snowmelt. From these stores, runoff is generated as a linear function of store size. The rate constants are set according to Thornthwaite and Mather (1957). The equations for rainfall-generated runoff are, for grid-cells where soil storage is at field capacity or above:

runoff from rainfall = 0.5{detention storage from rainfall
                  + p(rainfall + actual evapotranspiration
                  − potential evapotranspiration)}

and for grid-cells where water storage is below field capacity, and all water recharges the soil moisture store (none goes to runoff storage):

runoff from rainfall = 0.5(detention storage from rainfall)

In these equations, runoff is in mm/month, and p is the proportion of surplus water attributable to rain, defined as

$$p = \frac{\text{rainfall}}{(\text{rainfall} + \text{snowfall})}$$

A snowpack accumulates in a grid-cell whenever the mean monthly temperature drops below −1.0 °C. Snowmelt occurs above that temperature. A simple model of snowpack behaviour was devised. At elevations of 500 m and below, the entire snowpack (and any fresh snow) is melted by the end of the first month of snowmelt. At elevations above 500 m, the melting process takes two months, with half of the first month's snowpack persisting through the second month. Snowmelt recharges any deficit of soil moisture, and any excess is passed to a snowmelt store for eventual runoff. Following Thornthwaite and Mather (1957), grid-cells at elevations at 500 m or below will lose 10 per cent of this store in the first month of snowmelt, and in subsequent months the rate of loss will be 50 per cent per month. At higher elevations, grid-cells will lose 10 per cent in the first month, 25 per cent in the second month, and 50 per cent thereafter. Thus, the amount of runoff derived from snowmelt in grid-cells lying at or below 500 m is defined, for the first month of snowmelt, as

runoff from snowmelt = 0.1(detention storage from snowmelt + snowpack)

and for subsequent months of snowmelt as

runoff from snowmelt = 0.5(detention storage from snowmelt)

The amount of runoff derived from snowmelt in grid-cells above 500 m is computed using the following equations: for the first month of snowmelt

runoff from snowmelt = 0.1(detention storage from snowmelt + (0.5 × snowpack)

for the second month of snowmelt

runoff from snowmelt = 0.25(detention storage from snowmelt + snowpack)

and for subsequent months of snowmelt

runoff from snowmelt = 0.5(detention storage from snowmelt)

In all these snowmelt equations, storages are in mm and flows are in mm/month; the snowpack is expressed as mm of water.

The runoff derived from rain and snow is added to yield the total runoff for each grid-cell. This information is then fed into the water-transport model.

The Water-Transport Model

The water-transport model uses information on fluvial topology, linear transfer through river channels, and a simple representation of floodplain inundation to generate monthly discharge estimates for all grid-cells within a simulated catchment. The model was initially applied to the Amazon and Tocantins river system. This combined catchment accounts for almost a fifth of the world's discharge of freshwater. The simulated Amazon Basin comprises

1936 grid-cells covering 5 920 000 km^2; the Tocantins Basin adds another 315 grid-cells covering 960 000 km^2. The topology of the river networks was mapped by hand from a series of 1:1 000 000 Operational Navigation Charts covering the Amazon–Tocantins system.

Channel flow was represented by a linear reservoir model. Each grid-cell is seen as a store of water with a characteristic turnover time, t. Standard transfer coefficients (rate constants), k (defined as $1/t$), were assigned to all grid-cells and then modified according to geometry. The 'standard' transfer coefficient is associated with rivers draining grid-cells on a north–south or east–west axis. Modifications are made depending on the geometry of the influent and effluent streams. For instance, a grid-cell receiving an influent stream from the south-west and with an exit in the north-east corner would have the standard k value multiplied by 0.7 to accommodate the longer residence in that grid-cell. In the case of multiple tributaries, the turnover rate is weighted by the mean annual flow. In grid-cells with no upstream inputs, the turnover rate is halved. The fluvial transport model also predicts flood-plain inundation. Floodplain exchanges take place whenever the monthly discharge leaving a grid-cell exceeds a specified fraction of long-term mean annual flow. Above this fraction, and with increasing discharge, inundation is simulated by apportioning the potential net increase in grid-cell water storage between the channel itself and its associated floodplain. Floodplain discharge storage rises until the rate of grid-cell storage become negative. During the recession of a flood, the potential net decrease in grid-cell storage is accounted for by changes in channel and floodplain storage using the same apportionment as for rising water.

The complete water transport model comprises a set of simultaneous differential equations applied to each grid-cell. The accounting period is set at one month. All storages are measured in cubic metres and flows in cubic metres per month. For channel storage, S_c, the equation is:

$$\frac{dS_c}{dt} = \begin{matrix}\text{water}\\\text{from}\\\text{upriver}\end{matrix} - \begin{matrix}\text{water}\\\text{going}\\\text{downriver}\end{matrix} + \begin{matrix}\text{runoff}\\\text{from}\\\text{grid-cell}\end{matrix} + \begin{matrix}\text{water exchange}\\\text{between channel}\\\text{and floodplain}\end{matrix}$$

where water exchange between the floodplain and channel is positive when transfer is from the floodplain to the channel; for floodplain storage, S_f, the equation is

$$\frac{dS_f}{dt} = -\text{water exchange between channel and floodplain}$$

The components of these equations are defined as

$$\text{water going downriver} = kS_c$$

where k is a downstream transfer coefficient (per month);

$$\frac{\text{runoff from}}{\text{grid-cell}} = A\left(\frac{\text{runoff from}}{\text{rain}} + \frac{\text{runoff from}}{\text{snow}}\right) \times 0.01$$

where A is the area of a grid-cell (m^2);

$$\begin{array}{l}\text{water exchange} \\ \text{between channel} \\ \text{and floodplain}\end{array} = -r_f\left(\begin{array}{ccc}\text{water} & \text{water} & \text{runoff} \\ \text{from} & - \text{going} & + \text{from} \\ \text{upriver} & \text{downriver} & \text{grid-cell}\end{array}\right)$$

when the discharge of water going downriver is greater than, or equal to, the product of a flood initiation parameter, c_f (which defines the proportion of long-term mean annual flow required to invoke floodplain exchanges), and the mean annual downriver discharge, and

$$\text{water exchange between channel and floodplain} = 0$$

when the discharge of water going downriver is less than the product of a flood initiation parameter, c_f, and the mean annual downriver discharge. The coefficient r_f determines the ratio of potential volume change that is assigned to floodplain storage.

Discharge Predictions

The water-balance and water-transport equations were used in conjunction with the network topology to predict monthly discharges. The model was tuned using an unbiased estimator of performance relative to observed data. Tests showed that the best model performance was afforded by the following parameter values: $k = 20$, $c_f = 0.9$, and $r_f = 0.65$. These parameters defined a 'standard' scenario. The model successfully determined the timing and magnitude of discharge at various locations in the basins of the Amazon and Tocantins Rivers (Fig. 6.2).

This kind of model could be coupled to chemical models to predict global biogeochemical phenomena. For example, a monthly prediction of the soil moisture content of the South American continent could be used with known relations between soil denitrification and soil moisture to predict the loss of nitrous oxide and the total loss of nitrogen to the atmosphere. The excess

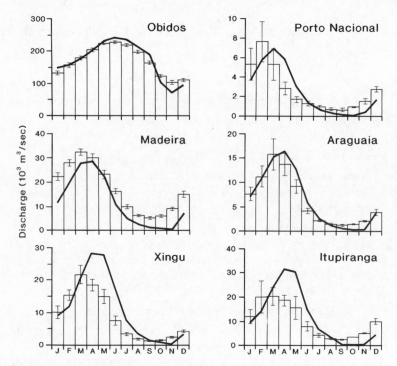

Note: Model predictions (lines) represent the best aggregate fit of the fluvial transfer and flooding coefficients.

Source: Vörösmarty et al. (1989: fig. 13).

FIG. 6.2. Predicted and observed discharge hydrographs for selected sites in the Amazon River system (Obidos, Madeira, and Xingu) and the Tocantins River system (Porto Nacional, Araguaia, and Itupiranga)

water in the water balance could be routed to stream channels, where it could be used to predict the discharge of the major rivers draining the continent. Changes in land use and the destruction of vegetation could readily be added to the models to permit the prediction of future changes in continental-scale biogeochemistry.

Forest Clearance and Rainfall

There is evidence that humans have changed the volume and composition of river flow. The stripping of the vegetation cover would be expected to reduce the transfer of water to the atmosphere by plant transpiration. It may be more than coincidence that since 1900 the global river flux has increased by 3 per cent (Probst and Tardy, 1987). Naturally, if deforestation increases river flux, then less water will be transferred back to the atmosphere, and it is possible that regional climates over extensive areas of deforested land might be altered. But, as with global warming, so with the water cycle: possible human-induced changes must be viewed against a background of natural changes. The increase in river flux during this century may have resulted from a protracted, global cycle of precipitation and evaporation. Separating natural changes from changes produced by human activity is an enormously difficult task. Nevertheless, models built to examine regional changes in the water cycle occasioned by forest clearance suggest that the human agency is causing some changes.

The source of much of the rain which falls over land areas in maritime and monsoon climates is water evaporated from the oceans. In Amazonia, it has been estimated that half the rain is derived from long-distance transport by the atmosphere and half from evapotranspiration within the basin. The large contribution of the Amazon Basin itself bespeaks long-term implications for rainfall patterns in the region as a result of forest destruction. The Amazon Basin contains about half the world's tropical forest. The pressure of a growing population, with attendant demands for increased crop production, for timber, and for firewood, have led to rapid deforestation.

To gauge the likelihood that the removal of the vegetation cover in the region will affect the Amazonian climate, Jennifer Lean and D. A. Warrilow (1989), using an atmospheric general circulation model, made a three-year simulation in which Amazon tropical forest and savanna is replaced by pasture. The model overcame some of the problems in earlier models used to assess the climatic impact of deforestation, which employed rather simple land-surface schemes of parameterization and lacked grid-scale data for good calibration. The model used a $2.5° \times 3.75°$ (latitude $\times$ longitude) grid and included a complex representation of interactive cloud processes. Land-surface parameterization included a four-layer soil temperature scheme. The land phase of the water cycle included interception of precipitation by a vegetation canopy, so permitting a zero resistance to re-evaporation and,

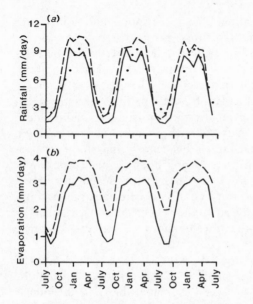

Note: Averaged over the region shown in the inset for 3 years starting in July. In both cases, the broken line represents the control simulation, the solid line the deforested simulation, and the dots the observed rainfall.

After Lean and Warrilow (1989).

FIG. 6.3. Monthly mean (*a*) precipitation (mm/day) and (*b*) evaporation (mm/day)

potentially, a more realistic partitioning of energy between latent heat fluxes and sensible heat fluxes. It also diagnosed runoff from the excess rainfall over infiltration capacity (accounting statistically for the spatial variability of rainfall) and subsurface runoff from the gravitational drainage of soil moisture.

Control and deforestation experiments were run over a three-year period. All grid-cells in South America north of 30°S defined as either tropical forest or savanna on a 1° × 1° grid were turned over to pasture. Soil characteristics, save infiltration capacity, were left unchanged. Looking at the results for the area in the southern part of Amazonia, where the largest change in land-surface characteristics occurred (Fig. 6.3 and Table 6.1), it can be seen that the control simulation is realistic (Table 6.1), despite that fact that it slightly amplifies the seasonal rainfall cycle (Fig. 6.3).

TABLE 6.1. *Summary of simulated and observed surface variables for the Amazon model*

Surface variable	Control simulation (3-yr mean)	Deforested simulation (3-yr mean)	% difference	Observations[a]
Evaporation (mm/day)	3.12	2.27	−27.2	3.34
Precipitation (mm/day)	6.60	5.26	−20.3	5.26
Soil moisture (cm)	16.13	6.66	−58.7	
Runoff (mm/day)	3.40	3.0	−11.9	2.76
Net radiation (W/m^2)	147.3	126.0	−14.5	
Temperature (°C)	23.6	26.0	+2.4	24.0
Sensible heat (W/m^2)	57.2	60.2	+5.2	
Bowen ratio[b]	0.85	1.5	+76.5	

[a] The observed values are difficult to compare with the simulation results because recordings are too sparse to give grid square means.
[b] The ratio of the sensible heat flux to the latent heat flux.

After Lean and Warrilow (1989: table 1, p. 412).

Acidification

The flux and storage of solutes in the biosphere is closely linked to the water cycle. Human activities have led to changes in the transfer, accumulation, and depletion of a range of solutes. The build-up of nutrients in lakes (eutrophication) was a decade or so ago a subject of investigation by mathematical models (see Huggett, 1980: 139–45). The latest environmental problem to attract large funds for research is acid rain and its effects on the environment.

As an example of a comprehensive model used to investigate the process of acidification in environmental systems, we shall take the Regional Acidification Information and Simulation model (RAINS), built by Joseph Alcamo and his colleagues (1987) at the International Institute for Applied Systems Analysis in Austria. This model was designed to test the effect of several different sulphur-reduction strategies on environmental systems. Separate submodels were constructed to deal with sulphur emissions, sulphur transport in the air, soil acidification, lake acidification, groundwater acidification, and the impact of forests. The model was spatially disaggregated, Europe being represented by grid-cells 150 × 150 km in size for the deposition submodel, and 0.5° × 1.0° (latitude × longitude) for the environmental-impact submodels. We shall describe each of these models in turn, save the last, which is not directly relevant to this chapter.

Emissions Model

The emissions of sulphur resulting from various economic sectors in twenty-seven European countries were computed according to a mass balance. The mass balance accounts for the energy consumed in each economic sector, together with fuel characteristics such as sulphur content, heat value, and the amount of sulphur retained by combustion. Five economic sectors were included: conversion (e.g. refineries), power plants, domestic, industrial, and transport; and eight fuels: brown coal, hard coal, derived coal (such as brown coal briquettes and coke), light oil (such as gasoline), medium distillate (gas oil), heavy oil, gas, and 'other fuels'. For each grid-cell, fuel type, and economic sector, sulphur emissions were determined by the following equation:

$$
\text{sulphur emissions} = \text{energy use} \left(\frac{\text{sulphur content}}{\text{heat value}} \right)
$$

$$
\times \left(\begin{array}{l} \text{fraction of} \\ \text{emissions not} \\ \text{retained in ash} \end{array} \right) \left(\begin{array}{l} \text{fraction of emissions} \\ \text{removed by} \\ \text{pollution control} \end{array} \right)
$$

$$
+ \left(\begin{array}{l} \text{sulphur emissions} \\ \text{from non-combustive} \\ \text{industrial processes} \end{array} \right)
$$

Atmospheric-Transport Model

Using information on sulphur emissions from each country, this model computed the concentration of sulphur dioxide in the air and the amount of sulphur deposited within Europe. It then added to the contributions from each country a background contribution to yield the total deposition rate of sulphur at all grid locations. Fig. 6.4 maps the sulphur deposition predicted by the model for various scenarios.

Soil-Acidification Model

The soil can, to some extent, buffer terrestrial and aquatic environmental systems against the inimical effects of acid deposition. It also acts as a regulator of acidification of surface waters and

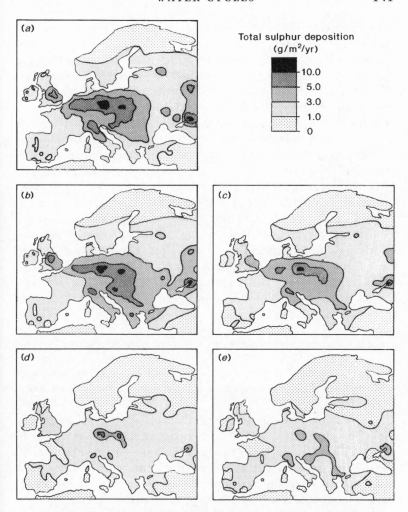

Total sulphur deposition
(g/m²/yr)

10.0
5.0
3.0
1.0
0

Note: (*a*) 1980. (*b*) 2000 according to a scenario in which no pollution control occurs. (*c*) 2000 according to a scenario in which sulphur emissions are reduced by 30% of their 1980 levels. (*d*) 2000 according to a scenario in which major sulphur controls are phased in from 1985 onwards. (*e*) 2000 according to a scenario which keeps the cost of controls low by setting a maximum deposition rate of 5 g/m²/yr within Europe.

After Alcamo *et al.* (1987).

FIG. 6.4. Maps of total sulphur deposition in Europe

groundwaters. The buffering capacity of soil stems from the production of base cations by weathering. So long as fresh supplies of cations are created by weathering at a rate exceeding the rate of acid deposition, then no acidification will take place. Where weathering cannot match the rate of acid deposition, the soil becomes progressively more acid in reaction; this is the process of soil acidification. In the RAINS model, the acidity of a 50-cm layer of soil was computed from the acid load (the input of protons to the soil) and the buffering characteristics of the soil. The acid load was worked out by assuming that all sulphur deposits are oxidized. Buffering characteristics are more complicated to define. They are divided into the buffer capacity, i.e. the total store of buffering compounds in the soil, and the buffer rate, i.e. the maximum potential rate of reaction between buffering compounds and acid load. These two factors needed to be included in the model because it is possible for a soil to have a high buffer capacity but have an acid reaction owing to a low buffer rate. The model was basically a storage equation for the cation-exchange capacity, CEC, of the soil:

$$\frac{dCEC}{dt} = \text{acid load rate} - \text{silicate weathering rate}$$

However, equations defining the equilibrium concentrations of hydrogen and aluminium ions in the soil were also, of necessity, included.

An example of the output from the soil model is shown in Fig. 6.5. This diagram depicts predicted soil acidity in forest soils of central European countries in the years 2000 (Fig. 6.5a) and 2040 (Fig. 6.5b) according to two scenarios: one which allows for a 30 per cent reduction of sulphur emissions from the 1980 levels; and a second in which major sulphur controls are effected. It is clear that forest soils in central Europe are commonly acidic, and that, as would be anticipated, the 30-per-cent-reduction scenario causes less of a rise in acidity than does the major-sulphur-controls scenario. The benefit of the major-sulphur-controls scenario is felt more fully by the year 2040 (Fig. 6.5b).

Lake-Acidification Model
Acidification of lakes in many mountainous and forested parts of Europe is a well-documented phenomenon. Estimates in Sweden

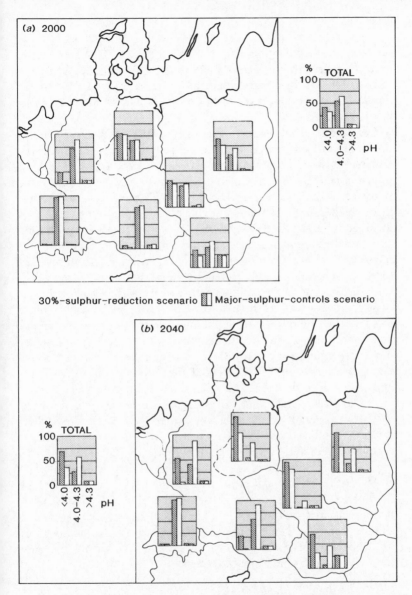

Note: (*a*) Predictions for the year 2000. (*b*) Predictions for the year 2040. In both diagrams, the bar charts show the aggregate distribution of soil acidity for all the countries shown.

After Alcamo *et al.* (1987).

FIG. 6.5. The predicted acidity classes of central European forest soils in pH classes for two scenarios—one in which sulphur emissions are reduced by 30% of their 1980 values, and a second in which major sulphur controls are phased in from 1985 onwards

suggest that acidification affects 15 000 of the 85 000 lakes larger than a hectare, and of these, 1800 are seriously affected. The party responsible for this lake acidification has proved tricky to pin down, but acidic runoff from soils with poor buffering capabilities is a likely candidate.

The acidity of lake water depends on many processes, including the amount of snowmelt, the route taken by runoff, lake chemistry, and many other chemical and physical processes. In the RAINS model, a lake catchment was represented by a snowpack store and two soil stores (a lower and an upper). Precipitation was routed through these stores. Water moving through the upper soil layer as pipeflow and fast throughflow comes into contact with humus and the upper mineral layers of the soil. Water moving through the lower soil layer can be thought of as slower throughflow. The ionic concentration in the moving water was calculated using the same method as in the soil acidification model. The contribution of soil water stores to the alkalinity of throughflow was assumed to equal the rate of weathering of base cations minus the incoming acid load. Change in the chemistry of lake water was predicted using an equilibrium expression for inorganic carbon species. Carbonate alkalinity was taken as the only significant buffering agent present in the lake, and to originate from processes going on in the lake catchment and processes going on in the lake itself.

An example of lake acidification predicted using the RAINS model is displayed in Fig. 6.6, which shows the acidity of lakes in regions of Finland, Sweden, and Norway in the year 2000 for the two sulphur-control scenarios. The acidity is presented as three acidity classes. Lakes in the class with pH less than 5.0 are dominated by acids, while those in the class pH 5.0–6.5 are poorly buffered, but not strongly acidified. Notice that the major-sulphur-controls scenario appreciably improves lake acidification in Sweden and Finland for the lowest acidity class; but generally the two scenarios have similar effects.

Groundwater-Acidification Model

The mechanisms underlying groundwater acidification are well known. However, quantifying the dynamic interactions between the relevant processes and the three-dimensional flow of groundwater on an inter-regional scale is a formidable task. The RAINS model ducks the problem by adopting a different approach.

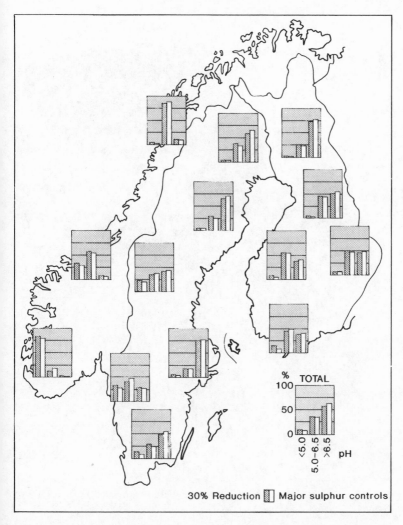

Note: The bar chart in the bottom right-hand corner of the diagram shows the aggregate distribution of the acidity for all lakes in the region.

After Alcamo *et al.* (1987).

FIG. 6.6. The predicted acidity classes of lakes in Finland, Norway, and Sweden for two scenarios—one in which sulphur emissions are reduced by 30% of their 1980 values, and a second in which major sulphur controls are phased in from 1985 onwards

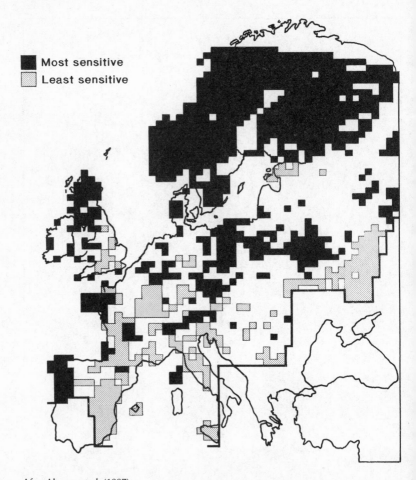

After Alcamo *et al.* (1987).

FIG. 6.7. A groundwater sensitivity map of Europe generated by a qualitative model

A map depicting the sensitivity of aquifers to acidification is produced by taking account of several variables, all of which are available for each grid-cell: soil base cation content, soil depth, soil texture; aquifer size and aquifer mineral composition; water available for recharge. The risk of groundwater to acidification was determined as a function of groundwater sensitivity (defined by a combination of all the above-mentioned variables) and the deposition of sulphur. Fig. 6.7 is a map of groundwater sensitivity generated by the model. It can be seen that northern and mountainous regions with thin soils and low weathering rates are the most sensitive to groundwater acidification; the deep-soiled agricultural areas are the least sensitive.

7

Life Cycles

The living systems of the biosphere perforce interact with their surroundings. Individuals and communities, by processes of natural selection, become adapted to the environment in which they live. Should that environment change, life systems must adapt, move elsewhere, or perish. We have seen that the human species, *Homo 'not-so-sapiens'*, is triggering massive environmental change on local, regional, and global scales. Simulations made with mathematical models suggest the change in communities and ecosystems which might arise during the next century in response to human perturbations of the biosphere. In this chapter, examples of these models will be described. First, we shall probe the stochastic models used to mimic the successional change in forests; second, we shall scrutinize two landscape models which simulate changes in complex ecosystems.

Vegetation and Global Warming

Communities are made up of large numbers of individual organisms belonging to numerous different species. The composition and structure of communities changes in the face of environmental perturbations. It is highly likely that during the next century many communities will be perturbed by greenhouse-gas-induced global warming. Several models have been built which try to predict the changes in vegetation occurring as the world warms up. Early work in this field indicated that, as a consequence of temperature changes associated with global warming, profound changes in the geography of plants and biomes would occur (e.g. Emanuel *et al.*, 1985). Later work, using forest growth simulation models, has unmasked the transient response of tree communities to climatic warming and to the accompanying changes in soil moisture stress and forest disturbance. We shall now explore some examples of this work.

Forest Dynamics in Eastern North America

The first attempt to model the transient response of vegetation to future changes in climate was made by Allen M. Solomon (1986). The model, called FORENA (Forests of Eastern North America), was a development of earlier forest succession models called JABOWA (Botkin *et al.*, 1972) and FORET (Shugart and West, 1977). It mimics forest succession in three stages: the establishment of new seedlings, the growth of the trees, and the death of the trees. And it keeps account of trees belonging to a maximum of seventy-two species in a stand with an area of 0.125 ha.

For each year in a simulation run, a cohort of seedlings is sown, the species composition and size of which is determined stochastically. The available species pool varies from one year to the next depending on the plot conditions, including light levels, the presence of leaf litter (related to the leaf area of the plot), the presence of mineral soil (related to the death of a large tree), and the death of a tree of a species capable of sprouting from roots when the above-ground parts are lost. The maximum growth achievable in a year by each tree under optimum conditions is computed according to a tree growth equation of the general form

$$\frac{dD}{dt} = \frac{gD\{1 - (Dh/D_{max}h_{max})\}}{(274 + 3b_2D - 4b_3D^2)}$$

where D is the diameter of the tree at breast height (cm), h is the height of the tree (cm), D_{max} and h_{max} are the maximum recorded diameters and height, respectively, for each tree species, and g, b_2, and b_3 are the growth rate parameters for each tree species (for derivation, see Shugart and West, 1977: 164–5). This optimal growth is reduced by multiplying the right-hand side by parameters for stand crowding, shade tolerance, temperature, and drought. Temperature is modelled as a stochastic variable: degree-days are fed into the model as sums of monthly random values drawn from predefined means and standard deviations. Winter cold temperatures (for January) are derived by a similar stochastic process. Drought days, too, are modelled stochastically. Lastly, for each simulated year, trees which die are selected at random according to an age-dependent mortality function and an age-independent mortality function. To make the model operational, parameters characterizing the limits to the establishment, growth, longevity, and mortality of each of the seventy-two species of tree are culled from silviculture manuals, and the values of the extrinsic variables, such as degree-days and drought days, are mapped using existing data sources.

Forest growth is simulated at twenty-one locations in eastern North America, as far west as a line joining Arkansas in the south to Baker Lake, Northwest Territories, in the north. The following special conditions are applied to each simulation run. All forests start growing on a clear plot and grow undisturbed for 400 years under a modern climate. After year 400, climate is changed owing to increased carbon dioxide levels in the atmosphere. A linear change of climate between years 400 and 500 is assumed, the new climate at year 500 corresponding to a doubling of atmospheric carbon dioxide levels. Climate continues to change linearly after year 500, so that, by year 700, the new climate corresponds to a quadrupling of atmospheric carbon dioxide levels. At year 700, climate stabilizes and the simulation proceeds for another 300 years. Simulation runs at each site are repeated ten times and the results averaged. Validation of the results is achieved by testing with independent forest composition data as provided by pollen deposited over the last 10 000 years and during the last glacial stage, 16 000 years ago.

Results for some of the sites are set out in Fig. 7.1. At the tundra–forest border, the response of the vegetation to climatic change is relatively simple (Fig. 7.1a). Basically, with four times the carbon dioxide in the atmosphere, the climate supports a much-increased biomass and, at least at Shefferville in Quebec, some birches, balsam poplar, and aspens. The response of northern boreal forest to warming is more complicated (Fig. 7.1b). With a fourfold increase in atmospheric carbon dioxide levels, the climate promotes the expansion of ashes, birches, northern oaks, maples, and other deciduous trees at the expense of spruces, firs, balsam poplar, and aspens. In all northern boreal forest sites, the change in species composition is similar, but takes place at different times. This underscores the time-transgressive nature of vegetational response to climatic change. The southern boreal forest and northern deciduous forest (Fig. 7.1c and d) also have a complicated response to climatic change. In both communities, species die back twice, the first time around and just after 500 years, and the second time from about 600 to 650 years.

In the southern boreal forest, the change is from a forest dominated by conifers (spruces, firs, and pines) to a forest dominated initially by maples and basswoods, and later by northern oaks and hickories. At some sites in the northern deciduous forest, species appear as climate starts to change then vanish once the stable climate associated with a quadrupled level of atmospheric carbon dioxide becomes established. Species which do this include the butternut (*Juglans cinerea*), black walnut (*Juglans nigra*), eastern hemlock (*Tsuga canadensis*), and several species of northern oak. In western and eastern deciduous forests, the response of trees to climatic warming is remarkably uniform between sites (Fig. 7.1e and f). Biomass declines everywhere, generally as soon as warming commences in the year 400. The drier sites in the west suffer the greatest losses of biomass, as well as a loss of species; this is to be expected as prairie vegetation would take over. The decline of biomass in the eastern deciduous forest probably results chiefly from the increased moisture stress in soils associated with the warmer climate. The increased moisture stress also gives a competitive edge to smaller and slower-growing species, such as the southern chinkipin oak (*Quercus muehlenbergii*), post oak (*Quercus stellata*), and live oak (*Quercus virginiata*), the black gum (*Nyssa sylvatica*), sugarberry (*Celtis laevigata*), and the American holly (*Ilex opaca*), which come to dominate the fast-growing species such as the American chestnut (*Castanea dentata*) and various northern oak species.

The Effect of Soil Water Regimes on Forest Dynamics

That the development of forests is assuredly influenced by the changes in soil water regimes resulting from global warming has been confirmed in a study made by J. R. Pastor and W. M. Post (1988). Using a population-based forest growth model (LINKAGES) and a soil process model, in conjunction with climate model predictions for a doubling of atmospheric carbon dioxide levels, these investigators probe the possible response of forests to global warming at several sites in the northeastern USA, including a site in northeastern Minnesota. The climate of this region is predicted to become warmer and drier. The major changes will occur at the boundary between the boreal forest and cool temperate forest. Forest growth is modelled on two soil types: soils with a high capacity to hold water and soils with a low capacity to hold water. The simulations begin in 1751. Bare plots

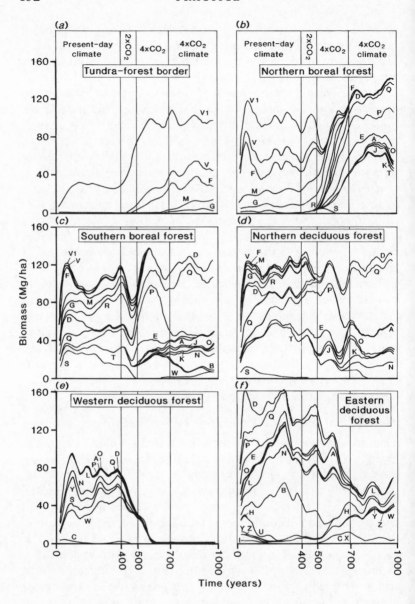

are 'sown' with seeds of the trees species common in the area. The model forest is then allowed to grow for 200 years under present climatic conditions. Next, carbon dioxide concentrations are gradually increased until, after a century, their present value has been doubled. After having reached that value, carbon dioxide levels are held constant for the next 200 years.

In brief, the model predicts that on soils with a high water-holding capacity, where there will be enough water available to promote tree growth, productivity and biomass will increase, but on soils with a low water-holding capacity, productivity and biomass will decrease in response to drier conditions. In turn, raised productivity and biomass will raise levels of soil nitrogen, whereas lowered productivity and biomass will lower levels of soil

Note: (a) Shefferville, Quebec (57° N, 67° W). (b) Kapuskasing, Ontario (49° N, 83° W). (c) West upper Michigan (47° N, 88° W). (d) North-central Wisconsin (45° N, 90° W). (e) South-central Arkansas (34° N, 93° W). (f) Central Tennessee (36° N, 85° W). The tree species are as follows: A. American beech (*Fagus grandifolia*); B. American chestnut (*Castanea dentata*); C. American holly (*Ilex opaca*); D. ashes: green ash (*Fraxinus pennsylvanica*), white ash (*Fraxinus americana*), black ash (*Fraxinus nigra*), blue ash (*Fraxinus quadrangulata*); E. basswoods: American basswood (*Tilia americana*) and white basswood (*Tilia heterophylla*); F. birches: sweet birch (*Betula lenta*), paper birch (*Betula papyrifera*), yellow birch (*Betula alleghaniensis*), and gray birch (*Betula populifolia*); G. balsam poplar (*Populus balsamifera*), bigleaf aspen (*Populus grandidentata*), trembling aspen (*Populus tremuloides*); H. black cherry (*Prunus serotina*); I. black gum (*Nyssa sylvatica*); J. butternut (*Juglans cinerea*) and black walnut (*Juglans nigra*); K. eastern hemlock (*Tsuga canadensis*); L. elms: American elm (*Ulmus americana*) and winged elm (*Ulmus alata*); M. firs: balsam fir (*Abies balsamea*) and Fraser fir (*Abies fraseri*); N. hickories: bitternut hickory (*Carya cordiformis*), mockernut hickory (*Carya tomentosa*), pignut hickory (*Carya glabra*), shagbark hickory (*Carya ovata*), shellbark hickory (*Carya laciniosa*), and black hickory (*Carya texana*); O. hornbeams: eastern hornbeam (*Ostrya virginiana*) and American hornbeam (*Carpinus caroliniana*); P. maples: sugar maple (*Acer saccharum*), red maple (*Acer rubra*), and silver maple (*Acer saccharinum*); Q. northern oaks: white oak (*Quercus alba*), scarlet oak (*Quercus coccinea*), chestnut oak (*Quercus prinus*), northern red oak (*Quercus rubra*), black oak (*Quercus velutina*), bur oak (*Quercus macrocarpa*), gray oak (*Quercus borealis*), and northern pin oak (*Quercus ellipsoidalis*); R. northern white cedar (*Thuja occidentalis*), red cedar (*Juniperus virginiana*), and tamarack (*Larix laricina*); S. pines: jack pine (*Pinus banksiana*), red pine (*Pinus resinosa*), shortleaf pine (*Pinus echinata*), loblolly pine (*Pinus taeda*), Virginia pine (*Pinus virginiana*), and pitch pine (*Pinus rigida*); and T. white pine (*Pinus strobus*); U. yellow buckeye (*Aesculus octandra*); V. spruces: black spruce (*Picea mariana*) and red spruce (*Picea rubens*), and V1 white spruce (*Picea glauca*); W. southern oaks: southern red oak (*Quercus falcata*), overcup oak (*Quercus lyrata*), blackjack oak (*Quercus marilandica*), chinkipin oak (*Quercus muehlenbergii*), Nuttall's oak (*Quercus nuttallii*), pin oak (*Quercus palustris*), Shumard's red oak (*Quercus shumardii*), post oak (*Quercus stellata*), and live oak (*Quercus virginiana*); X. sugarberry (*Celtis laevigata*); Y. sweetgum (*Liquidambar styraciflua*); Z. yellow poplar (*Liriodendron tulipifera*).

After Solomon (1986).

FIG. 7.1. Simulation of forest biomass dynamics over one millennium in response to climatic change induced by increasing levels of carbon dioxide in the atmosphere at six sites in eastern North America

nitrogen. The vegetation changes are, therefore, self-reinforcing. On water-retentive soils, global warming favours the expansion of northern hardwoods (maples, birches, basswoods) at the expense of conifers (spruces and firs); on well-drained, sandy soils, it favours the expansion of a stunted oak—pine forest, a relatively unproductive vegetation low in nitrogen, at the expense of spruces and firs.

Disturbance and Forest Dynamics

A study by Jonathan T. Overpeck, David Rhind, and Richard Goldberg (1990), using the results of climate models, shows that global warming would favour a rise in the rate of forest disturbance owing to an increase in weather conditions likely to cause forest fires (drought, wind, and natural ignition sources), convective winds and thunderstorms, coastal flooding, and hurricanes. Previous studies, such as that made by Solomon (1986), although acknowledging that disturbance could have an appreciable effect on forest composition, do not include it in the simulations.

The study made by Overpeck and his colleagues demonstrates that the response of forest biomass and composition to the change of climate associated with global warming is influenced by changes in disturbance. Their results uphold the view that the nature of forests could be changed radically by the first part of the next century. They use a FORENA model, modified so that the probability of disturbance of all trees on a given plot can be specified. Two sets of simulation are run. In the first set ('step function' experiments), simulated forest is grown from bare ground under present-day climate for 800 years so that the natural variability of the simulated forest can be characterized. At year 800, a single climatic variable is changed in a single step to a new mean value, which will perturb the forest, and the simulation is continued for a further 400 years. In each perturbation experiment, the probability of a catastrophic disturbance is changed from 0.00 to 0.01 at year 800. This is a realistic frequency of about one plot-destroying fire every 115 years when a 20-year regeneration period of the trees in a plot is assumed (during which no further catastrophe takes place). In each of the step-function simulations, three types of climatic change (perturbation) are modelled: a 1 °C increase in temperature; a 2 °C increase in

TABLE 7.1. *Sites chosen for forest simulations*

State or Province	Latitude (°N)	Longitude (°W)	Dominant modern-day forest trees
Northern Wisconsin	45.0	90.0	Pines, maples, oaks
Southern Quebec	47.9	75.0	Firs, spruces, birches
North-east Michigan	44.8	83.6	Pines, oaks, spruces
Southern Illinois	39.0	89.0	Oaks, hickories

After Overpeck *et al.* (1990: fig. 2, p. 52).

temperature; and a 15 per cent decrease in precipitation. In the second set of simulation runs ('transient' experiments), forest growth is, as in the step-function experiments, started from bare ground and allowed to proceed for 800 years under present climatic conditions. Then, from years 800–900, the mean climate, both temperature and precipitation, is changed year by year in a linear manner to simulate a twofold increase in the level of atmospheric carbon dioxide. From years 900–1600, the mean climate is again held constant. As in the step-function experiments, the probability of forest disturbance is changed from 0.00 to 0.01 at year 800. In all simulation runs, a relatively drought-resistant soil is assumed, and the results are averaged from forty random plots into a single time series for each model run.

The model is calibrated for selected sites in the mixed coniferous–hardwood forest of Wisconsin and the southern boreal forest of Quebec (Table 7.1). Selected summary results are presented in Fig. 7.2. It is apparent that an increase in forest disturbance will probably create a climatically induced change of vegetation that is equal to, or greater than, the same climatically induced change of vegetation without forest disturbance. In many cases, this enhanced change resulting from increased disturbance is created by rapid rises in the abundances of species associated with the early stages of forest succession owing to the increased frequency of forest disturbance. In some cases, as in Fig. 7.2*a*, *d*, and *e*, a step-function change of climate by itself does not promote a significant change in forest biomass; but the same change working hand in hand with increased forest disturbance does have a thoroughgoing effect on forest composition and biomass. Interestingly, the altered regimes of forest disturbance, as well as

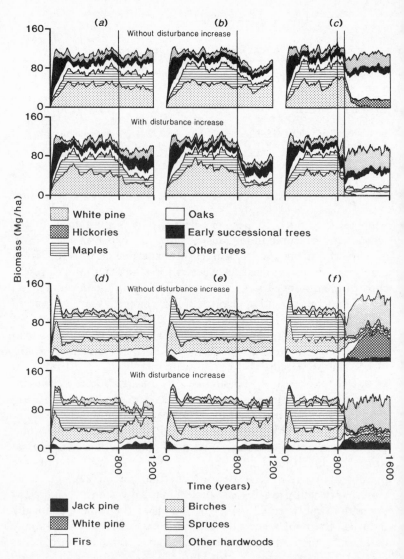

Note: (*a*)–(*c*) is a site in Wisconsin, and (*d*)–(*f*) a site in southern Quebec. At both sites, experiments were run with an increase in disturbance at year 800 (top figure for each site) and without an increase in disturbance at year 800 (bottom figure for each site). Additionally, three climatic change scenarios were simulated: a 1 °C temperature increase at year 800 (left-hand figures, *a* and *d*); a 15% decrease in precipitation (middle figures, *b* and *e*); and a transient change in which mean monthly precipitation and temperature were changed linearly from year 800 to year 900 and thereafter held constant (left-hand figures, *c* and *f*).

After Overpeck *et al.* (1990).

FIG. 7.2. Simulated changes in species composition of forests at two sites investigated in eastern North America

causing a change in the composition of the forests, also boost the rate at which forests respond to climatic change. For instance, in the transient climate-change experiments, where forest disturbance is absent through the entire duration of the simulation period, vegetation change lags behind climatic change by about 50–100 years, and simulated vegetation takes at least 200–250 years to attain a new equilibrial state. In the simulation runs where forest disturbance occurred from year 800 onwards, the vegetational change stays hard on the heels of climatic change, and takes less than 180 years to reach a new equilibrium composition after the climatic perturbation at year 800.

Landscape Systems

This section will discuss attempts to develop fully integrated models of ecological and landscape systems. Trustworthy predictions of human impacts on the environment can be obtained from sophisticated mathematical models which bring together the best available information on the dynamics of the abiotic and biotic components of environmental systems, and integrate them in such a way as to give an overall picture of the form and function of the entire landscape. It is now possible to predict changes in patterns of land cover across areas covering tens to hundreds of kilometres over time-spans of tens to hundreds of years resulting from specific human impacts. This degree of sophistication has been brought about by two developments: the ready accessibility of extensive spatial and temporal data bases from remote sensing, and the recent surge in computer power which enables models to be built at detailed levels of resolution. We shall look at two examples. The first is a moderately complex spatial model to simulate the impacts of a river diversion on bottomland forest communities in South Carolina; and the second is a very sophisticated spatial model of coastal landscape dynamics.

Bottomland Forests in the Santee River Floodplain

Leonard Pearlstine and his colleagues (1985) combined a forest growth model with a simple hydrological model to study the effect of the diversion of the Santee River, South Carolina, on the growth and succession of bottomland hardwood forest. The

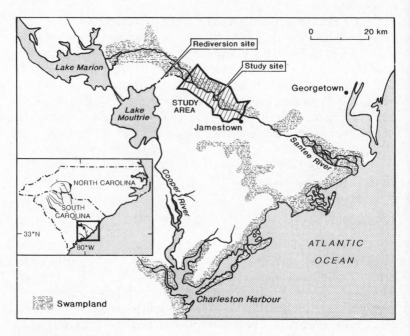

After Pearlstine *et al.* (1985).
FIG. 7.3. Location of the Santee River and proposed river diversion

coastal plain drainage of the Santee River was drastically modified
in 1941. Much of the Santee River discharge (88 per cent) was
diverted into the Cooper River as part of a hydroelectric power
project (Fig. 7.3). However, this diversion of water has led to
silting in Charleston Harbor, the main navigation channels
in which require year-round dredging. To alleviate this costly
problem, authorization was granted in 1968 to redivert most of
the water back into the Santee River via an 18.5-km canal feeding
off Lake Moultrie (Fig. 7.3). An additional hydroelectric power
plant would be constructed on this canal. Fears have been voiced
that this rediversion would inundate much of the Santee floodplain and cause a substantial decline in the bottomland forest.
After the diversion, the Santee River would return to 80 per cent
of its pre-diversion flow rate, with seasonal spates of floods and
stages of low flows. A crucial change would be a reduction of flow
early in the growing season.

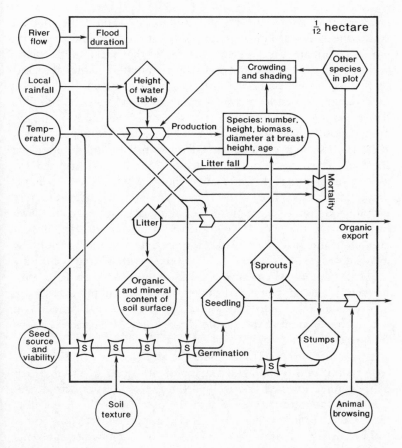

After Pearlstine *et al.* (1985).
FIG. 7.4. FORFLO forest floodplain succession model depicted in energese

In an effort to quantify the effects of the changed hydrological regime on the bottomland forests, a forest growth model was developed which allowed hydrological variables to influence tree species composition through seed germination, tree growth, and tree mortality. The forest growth model, called FORFLO, was a development of the FORET model. It is outlined in Fig. 7.4. Key points to note are the assumed relationships between flooding and various aspects of forest growth succession. First, for all tree species, save black willow and eastern cottonwood, seeds will not germinate when the ground is flooded. Should the plot be continuously flooded during that period of the year when a species would germinate, then the germination of that species fails. Black willow and eastern cottonwood can germinate whether the land be flooded or not. Secondly, after having germinated, the survival of seedlings depends on environmental conditions. A notable determinant of the seedling survival rate is the duration of the annual flood. Each species has a tolerance to flooding, and will survive if its range of tolerance falls within the flood duration for the plot. Thirdly, the optimum growth of trees was reduced by, among other things, a water table function which models flood-plain conditions. The water table function modifies the tree growth equation to account for the tolerance of species to the level of water on the plot during the growing season. The model computes the height of water for each half-month during the growing season. It is assumed that all trees will fail to grow during the half-months when they are more than three-quarters sub-merged by flood water. At lower levels of submergence, tree growth was related to water level by a curvilinear function in which the optimum water-table depth for each species is taken into account.

The model was used to simulate the effect of the proposed river rediversion, and a modified version of it, along a 25-km reach of the Santee forested floodplain from the rediversion site down-stream to Jamestown (Fig. 7.3). In the proposed rediversion, flow from Lake Marion to the Santee River stays the same, flow to the Cooper River is reduced to $85\,m^3/s$ (the level which prevents silting in Charleston Harbor), increasing the annual flow to the Santee River via the rediversion canal to $413\,m^3/s$. The modified rediversion was the same as the proposed rediversion except that, during the early growing season (April to July), flow through the rediversion canal was kept to a level which could be handled by just one of the three turbines at the power station. Although this would mean that the Cooper River would exceed the critical flow of $85\,m^3/s$ for the four months of the growing season, and thus cause some silting at the coast, it might promote the preservation of the bottomland forest.

The simulated responses of the forests to the rediversion are shown in Fig. 7.5. The annual duration of flooding appears to be a crucial factor in determining the course of vegetational

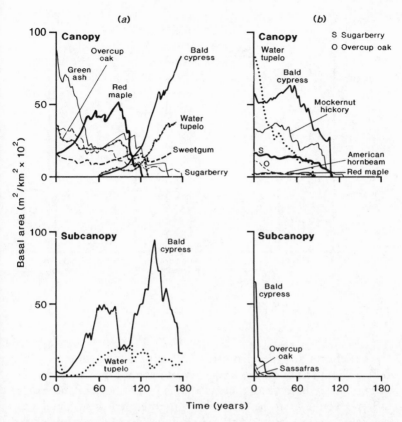

Note: (a) Bottomland forest community subjected to an annual flood duration of 45 ± 4%. (b) Bottomland hardwood community subjected to an annual flood duration of 72 ± 5%. The flood duration is the percentage of a year during which a plot is flooded. The plant species are named in Fig. 7.1 except the bald cypress (*Taxodium distichum*), water tupelo (*Nyssa aquatica*), and sassafras (*Sassafras albidum*).

After Pearlstine *et al.* (1985).

FIG. 7.5. Results of FORFLO simulations

change. With an annual flood duration in excess of 30–35 per cent (Fig. 7.5a), bottomland hardwood forest is replaced by cypress–tupelo forest, bald cypress and water tupelo being the only species which could manage to regenerate. When annual flood duration was above 65–70 per cent, no species was able to survive and the forest was replaced by a non-forest habitat; this happened more rapidly in the subcanopy.

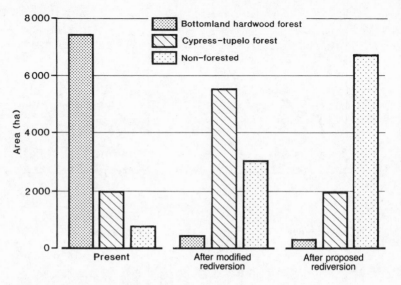

Data from Pearlstine *et al.* (1985: table 1).

FIG. 7.6. Changes in habitat in the study area of the Santee River

The effects of the proposed rediversion and the modified rediversion version on the frequency of habitat types are indicated in Fig. 7.6. In both cases there is a large loss of bottomland forest: a 97 per cent loss in the case of the proposed rediversion and a 94 per cent loss in the modified rediversion. The saving grace of the modified rediversion plan is that a forest cover is maintained: bottomland forest changes to cypress–tupelo forest, rather than open water. Assuming these predictions of sweeping changes in the bottomland forest along the Santee River to be trustworthy, then plainly it would be advisable to rethink the plans for rediverting the flow from the Cooper River.

A Coastal Ecosystem in Southern Louisiana

Ecosystems occupying coastal locations are under threat from a variety of human activities: gas and oil exploration, urban growth, sediment diversion, and greenhouse-gas-induced sea-level rise, to name but a few. To protect and preserve these ecosystems, it is valuable to know what the effects of proposed human activities are likely to be, and how these effects differ from natural changes.

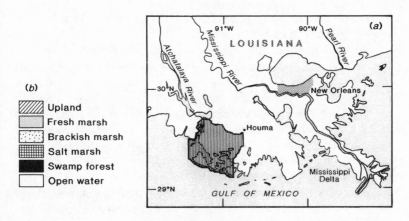

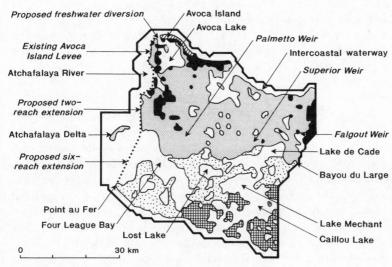

Note: (*a*) General location map. (*b*) Major geographical features, types of habitat in 1983, and management options considered in the simulations.

After Costanza *et al.* (1990).

FIG. 7.7. The Atchafalaya Delta and Terrebonne Parish marshes study area in southern Louisiana

In an effort to address these questions, Robert Costanza and Fred H. Sklar have built models of the dynamics of the Atchafalaya Delta and adjacent Terrebonne Parish marshes in southern Louisiana (Fig. 7.7). This landscape, part of the

Mississippi River distributary system, is one of the most rapidly changing landscapes in the world. The Atchafalaya River is one of the two principal distributaries of the Mississippi River, and carries about 30 per cent of the Mississippi discharge to the Gulf of Mexico. Over the last fifty years, sediments transported by the Atchafalaya River have been laid down in the bay area. In consequence, the bay area has gradually become filled in, and in 1973 a new subaerial delta appeared which has since grown and has an area of about $50 \, km^2$. Other changes are taking place in the area. The western Terrebonne marshes are becoming less salty, while the eastern part of the area is becoming more salty: the boundary between fresh and brackish marshes has shifted closer to the Gulf in the western marshes, and farther inland in the east (Fig. 7.8). As a whole, the study region is suffering loss of wetland, but rates of loss in the Terrebonne marshes has slowed and reversed over the past two decades owing to river deposition. The hydrology of the area has been greatly altered by dredging of waterways and the digging of access canals for petroleum exploration.

A Spatial Model of the Marsh-Estuarine System

To elucidate the effect that human activity has had on the coastal landscape system, a dynamic spatial model was developed and christened the Coastal Ecological Landscape Spatial Simulation (CELSS) model. The marsh-estuarine complex was divided into 2479 square grid-cells, each with an area of $1 \, km^2$. Each grid-cell stores water, suspended sediment, and bottom sediment, and exchanges water and sediment across each of its four sides. The flow of water across a side of a grid-cell was defined as a function of water storage, W, and flow connectivity, K. The water storage, W, is directly proportional to the height of water in a cell. Elevational gradients in the area are all low because of the flatness of the coastal marsh habitat. The overall water-flow connectivity, K, is a function of habitat type, drainage density, waterway orientation, and levee height. The change in water level in each grid-cell is determined in the model by water exchanges in both directions across all four grid-cell boundaries plus any exogenous input from surplus rainfall (precipitation less evapotranspiration). The rate of change in water level for a grid-cell was thus defined by a storage equation of the form (see Fig. 7.9 for notation):

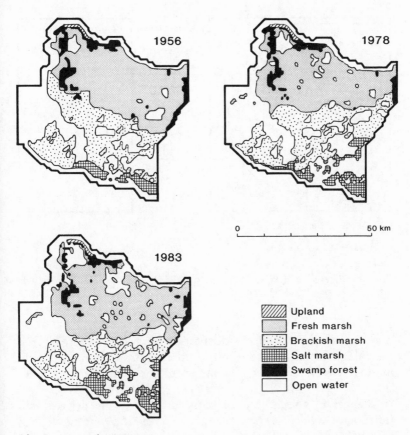

After Costanza *et al.* (1990).

FIG. 7.8. Observed distribution of habitats in the Atchafalaya–Terrebonne study area

$$\frac{dW_{i,j}}{dt} = (K_{i,j+1,i,j})(W_{i,j+1}) - (K_{i,j,i,j+1})(W_{i,j})$$
$$+ (K_{i,j-1,i,j})(W_{i,j-1}) - (K_{i,j,i,j-1})(W_{i,j})$$
$$+ (K_{i+1,j,i,j})(W_{i+1,j}) - (K_{i,j,i+1,j})(W_{i,j})$$
$$+ (K_{i-1,j,i,j})(W_{i-1,j}) - (K_{i,j,i-1,j})(W_{i,j}) + SR_{i,j}$$

where $K_{i,j+1,i,j}$ is the overall water-flow connectivity parameter from grid-cell $i,j+1$ to grid-cell i,j, and depends on habitat type,

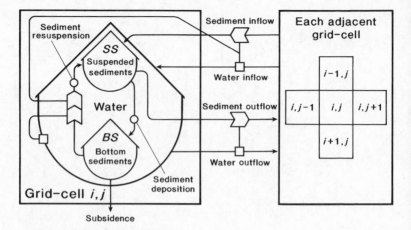

Note: Fluxes of suspended sediments are proportional to flows of water.

After Sklar and Costanza (1986).

FIG. 7.9. Storages and flows of water, suspended sediments, and bottom sediments for a typical grid-cell

drainage density, waterway orientation, and levee height; $W_{i,j}$ is the volume of water in grid-cell i,j (directly proportional to height in this system); and $SR_{i,j}$ is the surplus rainfall input to grid-cell i,j.

Changes in abiotic material concentrations were defined as a function of water flow between grid-cells and the concentration of materials in the cells. So, the storage equation for suspended sediment in a grid-cell is defined in the model as:

$$
\begin{aligned}
\frac{dSS_{i,j}}{dt} = & (J_{i,j+1,i,j})(SS_{i,j+1}) - (J_{i,j,i,j+1})(SS_{i,j}) \\
& + (J_{i,j-1,i,j})(SS_{i,j-1}) - (J_{i,j,i,j-1})(SS_{i,j}) \\
& + (J_{i+1,j,i,j})(SS_{i+1,j}) - (J_{i,j,i+1,j})(SS_{i,j}) \\
& + (J_{i-1,j,i,j})(SS_{i-1,j}) - (J_{i,j,i-1,j})(SS_{i,j}) \\
& - KSED(SS_{i,j}) + (TV)(JIN_{i,j})(BS_{i,j})
\end{aligned}
$$

where $dSS_{i,j}$ is the concentration of suspended sediment in grid-cell i,j; $J_{i,j+1,i,j}$ is the water flux from grid-cell $i,j+1$ to grid-cell i,j $(=K_{i,j+1,i,j})$ $(W_{i,j+1})$; $KSED$ is a sedimentation parameter; TV is a turbulence vector parameter; $JIN_{i,j}$ is the total water flux into grid-cell i,j; and $BS_{i,j}$ is the relative elevation of bottom sediments

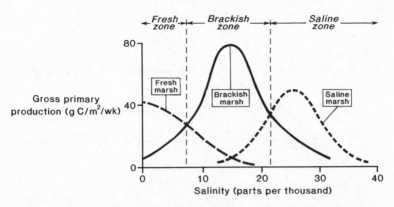

Note: The example shows the response of plant production to the salt content of water. The vertical arrows indicate the points at which habitats switch from one type to another in the CELSS model.

After Sklar and Costanza (1986).

FIG. 7.10. Plant primary production represented by Gaussian (normal distribution) curves

for grid-cell i, j. Material storage equations for other abiotic components of the system—salts, nutrients, and bottom sediments—were handled in a similar fashion. So, too, were the water-borne transport elements of biotic components.

Changes in the biotic components in grid-cells depended on abiotic states and habitat type of the cells. Primary production was simulated using a Gaussian distribution function, one function being defined for each habitat and each abiotic state variable. Fig. 7.10 shows plant-productivity functions for salinity in three habitats. Nutrient uptake was simulated using appropriate Michaelis–Menten rate equations, as depicted in Fig. 7.11. The complex interactions between primary production and the supply of nutrients (in this case, nitrogen) was modelled according to the schedule in Fig. 7.12. It can be seen that factors influencing the dissolved nitrogen concentration include denitrification, Michaelis–Menten uptake, deposition, rain and river inputs, subsidence, and hydrological exports. Under optimum conditions, primary production is maximized and large quantities of organic matter accumulate in the sediments. In turn, this process maintains the elevation of the land by balancing fall caused by subsidence.

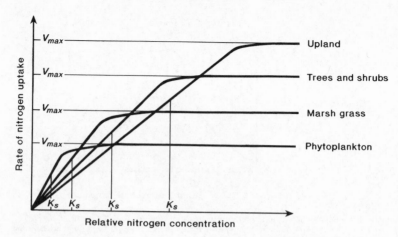

Note: The example depicted here shows nitrogen uptake. V_{max} is the maximum rate of uptake for a given habitat and K_s is the corresponding half-saturation constant.

After Sklar and Costanza (1986).

FIG. 7.11. The uptake of nutrients in the CELSS model is defined as a function of habitat type and nutrient concentration

The model allows habitat succession to occur: after a time lag, one habitat becomes more like another owing to changing conditions. The computer programme monitors the state variables in each grid-cell, checking if the physical environment (salinity, elevation, water, and so forth) be stable. Should the state variables change to such an extent that the environment of a grid-cell no longer conforms to the state of its designated habitat, then all parameters in the cell switch to settings representative of the cell's new environment. In other words, the habitat type is changed.

Calibrating the Spatial Model

A big problem with large-scale landscape models of this sort is finding enough field data with which to calibrate and test the model. For the Atchafalaya–Terrebonne region, some spatial data exist: habitat maps for 1956, 1978, and 1983; field measurements of water levels, plant production, salinity, nutrient concentrations, and so on, taken over a number of years; and the results of hydrodynamic models. For the period of simulation—1956–78, in early runs, and 1956–83 in later runs—forcing functions were specified as boundary conditions in the form of time series.

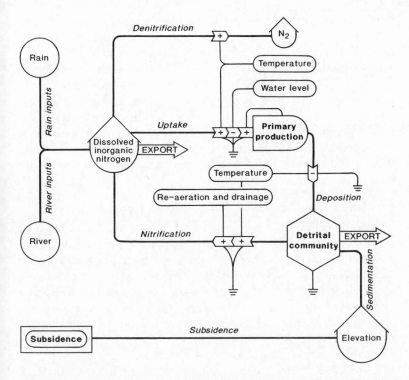

Note: Physical and biological processes control the storage and exchange rates of dissolved inorganic nitrogen.

After Sklar and Costanza (1986).

FIG. 7.12. The interactions between primary production and the supply of nutrients (in this case nitrogen) in the CELSS model

Weekly values of Atchafalaya River and Mississippi River discharges, Gulf salinity, river sediments and nutrients, rainfall nutrients, sea level, runoff, temperature, and air movement were fed in at each iteration of the simulation.

The location and characteristics of all the waterways were also incorporated into the model. This was important, since waterways and their characteristics significantly affect water flow. They were added to the model in the form of digitized maps of waterways and levees. In addition to overland flow, water may move from one grid-cell to another via canals or natural bayous. Conversely, water is prevented from crossing cell sides by levees. The overall flow connectivity parameter, K, is thus adjusted to reflect the presence and size of waterways or levees at the grid-cell boundaries. If a waterway is present at a grid-cell boundary, a large K value is used, increasing with the size of the waterway; if a levee is present, a K value of 0 is used until the water level exceeds the levee height. The canal and levee network is updated each year during a simulation run. All the above-mentioned conditions define the base case. In later runs, with a view to looking at possible future changes in the region resulting from climatic change and proposed management schemes, driving variables and other parameters were changed.

Simulating Landscape Change in the Marsh-Estuarine System

The original base-case run lasted twenty-four years and engaged some 1248 weekly iterations. With eight state variables and with different habitat types available for each of the 2479 grid-cells, the quantity of output was enormous. The best way of appreciating the predicted change of the system would be to use a video camera to animate a time series of the weekly maps of the variables. All that can be shown here are a few snapshots of some of the simulated changes.

Example output from a base-case run, which covered the period 1956 to 1983, is mapped in Fig. 7.13. Model predictions for 1978 and 1983 are shown for habitat, water volume, suspended sediments, and salinity. The actual habitat types observed in each grid-cell in 1956 (the initial conditions), 1978, and 1983 have already been presented in Fig. 7.8. The model accurately reproduced the slow intrusion of salty water from the south-eastern part of the study area, and the concomitant freshening of water in the south-western sector which resulted from an increase in the freshwater input from the Atchafalaya River. Elevation (not illustrated) is predicted to have decreased in the north of the area and increased in the south of the area. The predicted changes in salinity and elevation are indicative of river water and sediments moving further south in recent times, and a lack of connectivity with the more northern fresh marsh areas due to levee construction. Predicted water volume and suspended-sediment patterns follow a similar course, and are broadly in line with the known historical behaviour of the variables in the area. These changes in the physical environment are predicted to have had repercussions

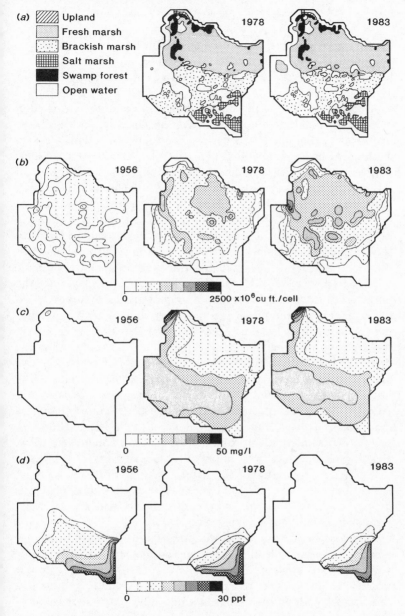

Note: The starting state in 1956 is also shown. (*a*) Predicted habitat types. (*b*) Water volume (millions of cubic feet per grid-cell). (*c*) Suspended sediments (milligrams per litre). (*d*) Salinity (ppt).

After Costanza *et al.* (1990).

FIG. 7.13. Maps of the values of selected state variables predicted by the CELSS model for 1978 and 1983

on the biotic ecosystem components. The dual effect of abiotic and biotic interactions has been a change in the predominant habitat of some grid-cells. These habitat changes can be seen in Fig. 7.13.

A telling feature of the CELSS model is its ability to predict changes of habitats under a range of climatic, management, historical, and boundary scenarios. The results of several scenario analyses, which predicted changes to the year 2033, are summarized in Table 7.2. Climate scenarios take 'climate' to mean all the driving variables including rainfall, Atchafalaya River flow, wind, and sea level. They address the impact of climatic changes on the study area. Management scenarios look at the effect of specific manipulations of the system by humans. Historical scenarios consider what the system would have been like had not the environment been altered by human action, and if climatic conditions had been different. Boundary scenarios delve into the potential impacts of natural and human-induced variations in the boundary conditions of the system, such as sea-level rise. The management and boundary scenarios were run by restarting the model with the actual habitat map for 1983, rather than the predicted habitat map for that year, to add more realism. Climate and historical scenarios were run starting in 1956, so that the full impacts of climate and historical variations could be assessed. After 1978, the rate of canal and levee construction for oil and gas exploration slowed appreciably compared with 1956–78, so all scenarios assumed that no canals or levees were built after 1978, except those specifically mentioned in the scenarios.

It is clear from Table 7.2 that the assumptions made about climatic change have a big influence on the distribution of habitats in the year 2033. The mean climate scenario, wherein the long-term average for each variable was used for all weeks, produced a modest loss in land area. On the other hand, the weekly average climate scenario, wherein each weekly value of each climatic variable for the entire run from 1956 to 2033 was set to the average value for that week in the 1956–83 data, produced a drastic loss of land area. This finding indicated that the annual flood cycle and other annual cycles in climatic variables are important to the land-building process, but that chance events, such as major storms and floods, tend to have a net erosional effect on marshland. If the global climate becomes less predictable

TABLE 7.2. Area (km²) occupied by each habitat type for three years for which data are available, and for 2033, under various scenarios

	Swamp	Fresh marsh	Brackish marsh	Saline marsh	Upland	Total land	Open water
Survey data							
1956	130	864	632	98	13	1737	742
1978	113	766	554	150	18	1601	878
1983	116	845	347	155	18	1481	998
Climate scenarios							
Base case[b]	84	871	338	120	10	1423	1056
Mean climate	94 (+10)[a]	974 (+103)	402 (+64)	136 (+16)	11 (+1)	1617 (+194)	862 (−194)
Weekly average climate	128 (+44)	961 (+90)	813 (+475)	300 (+180)	11 (+1)	2213 (+790)	266 (−790)
Management scenarios							
No levee extension	100	796	410	123	15	1444	1035
Full six-reach levee extension	103 (+3)	790 (−6)	362 (−48)	122 (−1)	15 (0)	1393 (−52)	1087 (+52)
Freshwater diversion	103 (+3)	803 (+7)	404 (−6)	123 (0)	15 (0)	1448 (+4)	1031 (−4)
Boundary scenarios							
Low sea-level rise[c]	104 (+4)	800 (+4)	411 (+1)	124 (+1)	15 (0)	1454 (+10)	1025 (−10)
High sea-level rise[d]	89 (−11)	794 (−2)	396 (−14)	131 (+8)	15 (0)	1425 (−19)	1054 (+19)
Historical scenarios[e]							
No original Avoca levee	84	951	350	126	13	1524	955
No effects	130	863	401	144	12	1550	929

[a] Brackets indicate changes from the base case.
[b] This is the base case for the management scenarios.
[c] 50-cm rise by the year 2100.
[d] 200-cm rise by 2100.
[e] No comparisons with a base case are given for the historical scenarios because these runs started in 1956 rather than 1983.

After Costanza et al. (1990: table 2, p. 102).

in the future as a result of global warming, then the stability of coastal marshes may be in jeopardy.

Several management scenarios were run. As the data in Table 7.2 indicate, the largest loss of land would arise from the full six-reach levee extension scheme which had been considered at one time. With this scheme, $48 \, km^2$ of brackish marsh and $6 \, km^2$ of fresh marsh would be lost by 2033, largely because the extended levees prevent sediment-laden water reaching the brackish marsh bordering Four League Bay, where most of the loss occurs. Boundary scenarios considered the effects of projected rates of sea-level rise, both high and low projections, on the area. The results were unexpected. Doubling the rate of eustatic sea-level rise from 0.23 to 0.46 cm/yr actually caused a net gain in land area of $10 \, km^2$ relative to the base case. This is probably because, so long as sediments loads are high, healthy marshes can keep pace with moderate rates of sea-level rise.

Two historical scenarios were tested: first, the changes in the system which might have taken place had not the original Avoca Island levee been built; and second, the changes which might have ensued had the Avoca levee or any of the post-1956 canals not been constructed. The results shown in Table 7.2 suggest that the original levee and the canals had a major influence on the development of the system, causing a far greater loss of land than would have occurred in their absence.

PART III
Prospects

8

The Role of Modelling

This short introduction to the mathematical modelling of the human impact on the environment will conclude by reviewing the current status and future possibilities on the modelling front and considering the role in modelling that should be taken by that adaptable breed of generalist—the geographer.

Modelling: The State of the Art

A new era of mathematical modelling has dawned in the last few years. This era was heralded by three developments: the inclusion of spatial dynamics, as well as purely temporal dynamics, into models of environmental systems; the accessibility of time series from remotely sensed images; and the advent of supercomputers and parallel processing. The development of spatial models was made possible by the developments in computing and geographical information systems derived from remotely sensed data: spatial models require the kind of grid-based data provided by remote sensing for input and for testing, and the power of the latest generation of computers to cope with the sheer number of calculations involved within a reasonable time. It is fortunate indeed that sophisticated, dynamical spatial models have appeared at a time when the need for a better understanding of the functioning of environmental systems is pressing.

Spatial Models

Over the last decade or so, there has been a burgeoning awareness of the significance of the spatial dimension in comprehending the behaviour of systems in general, and of environmental systems in particular. The first signs that the explicit inclusion of spatial variables in system state equations would make a difference to the system dynamics came in early simulations of ecological systems in the late 1950s, though spatial models in geography and fluid

TABLE 8.1. *Some mathematical models which tackle spatial problems*

Discipline and type of model	Modelling objective	Typical variables used
Geography		
Geometrical	Establish relations between form variables	Shape, size, direction, distance
Demographic	Predict movement of people between regions	Births, deaths, population density, information
Network	Minimize cost of movement between points in a network	Production, consumption, rates of flow
Fluid dynamics		
Hydrodynamics	Predict velocity and mass distribution in a spatial field of a fluid	Distance, momentum, acceleration, friction
General circulation	Predict velocity, direction, and mass of flows in the atmosphere–ocean system	Distance, density, pressure, temperature, turbulence, water vapour, salinity
Ecology		
Population	Predict the size of populations	Births, deaths, migration, population density, resources
Ecosystem	Predict resource distribution and the size of several populations	Births, deaths, migration, population density, resources
Landscape ecology		
Stochastic	Predict changes of state in a spatial system	Distance, habitat type, density, state transition rates
Deterministic (Process based)	Predict storage, transfers, and transformations in a spatial system	Mass, density, births, deaths, movement rates, momentum, resources

After Sklar and Costanza (1991: table 10.4, pp. 275–6).

dynamics had existed well before that time. When spatial variables were added to the classic Lotka–Volterra predator–prey equations, it was found that the dynamics of the system were radically altered. Spatial models have emerged, virtually independently, in several disciplines (Table 8.1). The most sophisticated spatial models, which lie at the very heart of human–environment interactions, are models of landscape ecology (see M. G. Turner, 1989).

Of recent origin, landscape ecology models are used to predict change in entire landscapes and to link landscape change at local, regional, and global scales. At least, such is the hope. All-inclusive landscape models are still in the early stages of development. An immediate aim is to assemble models which relate biotic components of ecosystems to regional and global models of the atmosphere and hydrosphere: the model devised by Charles Vörösmarty and his colleagues, discussed in Chapter 6, takes a step in this direction. The ultimate aim of such endeavour is to create global biosphere–geosphere models that enable us to appreciate more deeply the impact of human activities on the environment. At present, the best simulators of landscape change are the process-based landscape ecology models, such as the Coastal Ecosystem Landscape Spatial Simulation model built by Robert Costanza and his colleagues and described in Chapter 7. These models are convincingly realistic: spatial variables are included explicitly, and cause-and-effect links are represented by a rich web of interactions. They hold out much promise as effective tools of global and regional environmental management.

Supercomputers

Supercomputers have allowed the formulation of very complex, spatially detailed models, including the later generations of general circulation model. Starting from serial machines in which a single processor interacts with a single memory, advances in computer technology have produced vector processor computers which use pipelined functional units fed from a vector register and, most recently, vector processor computers with multiple processors.

Used in conjunction with parallel processors, supercomputers greatly shorten the time needed to manipulate exceedingly large and realistic arrays of spatial data. They allow data to be integrated, the effects of competing processes to be sorted, and natural scales of distance and time to be maintained. In addition, they offer superb facilities for displaying spatially detailed information generated in simulation runs. Craig M. Bethke and his colleagues (1988), for example, used supercomputers to analyse the development of fluid transport and chemical reactions, and especially the development of fluid pressures in the rocks, in the Gulf of Mexico sedimentary basin. Part of the output was a three-dimensional rendition of predicted fluid pressures in rocks of the Gulf Basin over the last 150 million years. Another example of a model which used a powerful vector processor computer, and the terrific colour graphics facilities linked with it, is the Fine Resolution Antarctic Model, which simulated the circulation of water in the southern oceans using a grid network fine enough to accommodate medium-scale eddies and major ocean currents (Webb, 1991).

Invaluable though supercomputers and other high-powered mainframe computers be to environmental modellers, the humble personal computer should not be undervalued. Modern PCs are relatively cheap and powerful, with excellent graphics facilities. Most of the models described in the previous chapters could be run on PCs. Indeed, PC versions of the IMAGE model (Rotmans, 1990) and the latest reincarnation of the JABOWA model (Botkin, 1992) are available on floppy disks. An exception is the general circulation models, which require vast amounts of storage, although package programmes of simple climate models are available (e.g. Henderson-Sellers and McGuffie, 1987). To be sure, much can be learnt about the principles of modelling and about the dynamics of environmental systems by experimenting with modelling packages (or self-written programmes) on personal computers. Try it!

Model Calibration

Most models, and expressly spatial models, are data-hungry: their calibration necessitates information on several variables for each grid-cell in the spatial domain under consideration. To provide this information from ground surveys is nigh on impossible, especially where the model covers inaccessible terrain. In some cases, existing maps of vegetation, soils, climatic variables, and so on have been used to calibrate spatial models. This was the case with the Osnabrück Biosphere Model. Basically, grids of the required density are superimposed on the maps, and the dominant 'state' of particular variables measured. A drawback with this practice is the need to interpolate data. For instance, climate is measured at points (meteorological stations), whereas the climatic variables needed in the calibration of a model must be fitted to all grid-cells, whether or not they contain a meteorological station. All mapped data are to a degree interpolated. They also tend to provide a sort of composite 'snapshot', a picture of the varying conditions within the region being modelled which is sketched from scraps of information gathered in various surveys carried out over several years or even decades.

Far more valuable are the data gleaned from remotely sensed images. These data are, normally, readily fitted to any grid size above a minimum level of spatial resolution, and each pixel in an image can be made to correspond to a grid-cell. Remotely sensed images provide complete coverage of the spatial domain of the system at a particular time. In some cases, images may be available for different times of year and for different years. This source of environmental data is a boon to modellers. As an example, look at the vegetation map of North America charted by Elaine Matthews from remotely sensed data (Fig. 8.1). This kind of information is invaluable in calibrating climate models. The use of geographical information systems in modelling is becoming commonplace and has made possible the calibration and testing of complex dynamic spatial models (e.g. Kessell, 1975; Moore *et al.*, 1991).

Limitations

Mathematical modelling has undoubtedly proved its worth over the last couple of decades. It has shown itself to be a flexible process adaptable to a variety of environmental systems. At the same time, it is firmly founded upon a base of substantial theory. But we have sung enough praises for mathematical models. At this juncture, it would be prudent to temper our extolment of modelling with a few cautionary remarks about the limitations of models. In this regard, there are two broad classes of limitation which need discussing.

First, there are practical limitations which need careful attention. They are not so much insuperable problems as technical difficulties. Prominent amongst them are the care which needs to be taken in the conceptual stage of model development, in the way of subdividing a spatial domain, and in the choice of mathematical methods for solving the system equations. The first and third of these considerations were discussed earlier in the book; the second has only been touched upon but should not be overlooked. When building a spatial model, it is important to ponder over the method of establishing spatial units. There is no correct way of chopping space into blocks. None the less, when doing so, it

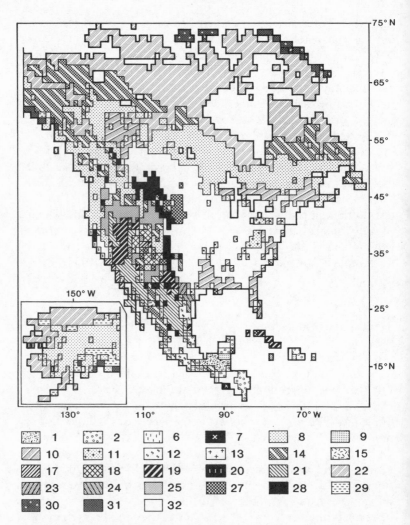

Note: The 32 ecosystems are: 1. tropical evergreen forest, mangrove forest; 2. tropical and subtropical evergreen broad-leaved forest; 3. subtropical evergreen rain forest; 4. temperate and subpolar evergreen rain forest; 5. temperate evergreen seasonal broad-leaved forest with summer rain; 6. evergreen broad-leaved sclerophyllous forest with winter rain; 7. tropical and subtropical evergreen needle-leaved forest; 8. temperate and subpolar evergreen needle-leaved forest; 9. tropical and subtropical drought-deciduous forest; 10. cold deciduous forest, with evergreens; 11. cold deciduous forest, without evergreens; 12. xeromorphic forest and woodland; 13. evergreen broad-leaved sclerophyllous woodland; 14. evergreen needle-leaved woodland; 15. tropical and subtropical drought-deciduous woodland; 16. cold deciduous woodland; 17. evergreen broad-leaved shrubland and thicket, evergreen dwarf shrubland; 18. evergreen needle-leaved or microphyllous shrubland and thicket; 19. drought-deciduous shrubland and thicket; 20. cold deciduous subalpine and subpolar shrubland, cold deciduous dwarf

should be borne in mind that the grid-cells (or polygons) should be of a size appropriate to the problem in hand: it would be pointless to use a grid so coarse that it missed significant spatial differences in state variables. The problem of setting up spatial units in general, and determining grid size in particular, is discussed by Heinrich Rohdenburg (1989), to which paper the reader is directed. Another practical matter to consider when building a model is deciding on the goals of the modelling experiments: is the aim realism, precision, or generality? All three goals cannot be realized at once. Models used in environmental management, such as the Coastal Ecosystem Landscape Spatial Simulation model devised by Robert Costanza and his colleagues, generally opt for high realism and precision. Models tackling more general issues tend, naturally, to go for greater generality. Where modelling is concerned, the means must be tailored to the ends.

The second class of modelling limitation has a philosophical character and is the greatest source of criticism of the systems approach. The key issue here is the failure to take on board different philosophical stances over the relationships between humans and nature, that is, the basic strands of modern environmentalist thought. There are several radically different philosophies of the environment which tend to polarize around, at one extreme, ecocentrism (Gaianism and communalism) and, at the other extreme, technocentrism (accommodationism and cornucopianism) (see O'Riordan, 1988). It is not possible or appropriate to enlarge upon these fascinating matters here. There is simply not room in the book, nor does the author have the expertise, to delve into policy-making aspects of environmental problems. Suffice it to say that mathematical models at least provide one way of establishing the likely consequences of implementing the environmental strategies advocated by the different groups of environ-

shrubland; 21. xeromorphic shrubland and dwarf shrubland; 22. arctic and alpine tundra, mossy bog; 23. tall, medium, and short grassland with 10–40% woody tree cover; 24. tall, medium, and short grassland with less than 10% woody tree cover or tuft-plant cover; 25. tall, medium, and short grassland with shrub cover; 26. tall grassland, no woody cover; 27. medium grassland, no woody cover; 28. meadow, short grassland, no woody cover; 29. forb formations; 30. desert; 31. ice; 32. cultivated land.

After Matthews (1983).

FIG. 8.1. Land-cover map of North America showing detailed subdivisions of major ecosystems in a 1° × 1° (longitude × latitude) grid

mentalists: they predict possible environmental consequences of certain human actions.

What should be done by governments and other decision-making bodies in the light of these predictions is a subject which justifies a book of its own (see e.g. Berry, 1992; Caldwell, 1990; Mintzer, 1992). But the uncomfortable fact is that those with the power to avert undesirable regional and global environmental changes generally take scant regard of the warnings of the modellers. At the time of writing, as the Earth Summit to be held at Rio de Janeiro in June 1992 approached, President George Bush was putting the self-interest of the United States before the interests of all nations of the world by ignoring the grim predictions of climate models and allowing global warming to proceed virtually unchecked, purely so that American economic growth would be unhampered.

Modelling: The Geographer's Role

With the surge of interest in spatial environmental systems, one would imagine that geographers might at last reinstate themselves as the explorers *par excellence* of people–environment interactions. This, however, appears not to be the case. Given that the present book is written chiefly for young geographers, it behoves its author, himself a geographer, to conclude by importuning his student audience to take up the challenge of modelling. His entreaty will explain why, with a few notable exceptions, geographers have so far abjured mathematical modelling, and why such an eschewal is foolish.

Traditionally, geographers have claimed matters spatial in the terrestrial sphere as their *raison d'être*. Also, they have been regarded, usually disparagingly, as jacks and jills of all trades. It would be more charitable, and nearer the truth, to say that geographers tend to possess eclectic minds. Given their keen, some might say obsessive, interest in spatial systems, and their catholicity, geographers seem admirably placed to occupy the van of the army of modellers attacking the weighty issues concerning the interactions between people and their environment. Many geographers do write on environmental issues. One has only to list books by geographers which have appeared in recent years to confirm this claim: Ian G. Simmons's *Changing the Face of the*

Earth: Culture, Environment, History (1989), Antoinette M.
Mannion's *Global Environmental Change: A Natural and
Cultural Environmental History* (1991), Andrew Goudie's *The
Human Impact on the Natural Environment* (1990), and the
massive volume edited by B. L. Turner and his colleagues, *The
Earth as Transformed by Human Action: Global and Regional
Changes in the Biosphere over the Past 300 Years* (1990). Nevertheless, compared with the population of geographers with a keen
interest in environmental problems, the number who are active on
the modelling front is tiny. Most modelling of global and regional
environmental systems is carried out by specialists in departments
of atmospheric science, ecology, Earth sciences, and applied
systems sciences.

Geographers, then, are in a curious position. The core of their
discipline is the interaction between the human species and its
environment; yet some of the giant scientific strides in this topical
area are being made by non-geographers. And, to add insult to
injury, many of the calibration techniques used in complex spatial
models are borrowed from geography. There is little doubt that
geographers have only themselves to blame for their position.
Non-geographers have not striven to usurp the geographer's role.
Rather, a niche was vacant, and, by and large, geographers were
not, and still are not, willing to fill it. This is a great loss to
geography and, because of the special expertise which geographers
have in the field of spatial systems and environmental philosophy,
to environmental science as well. Without wishing to belittle the
achievements of environmental scientists, geographers are better
versed in questions of spatial systems, generally more knowledge-
able about philosophical issues of environmentalism, and better
placed to explore the interface between social, cultural, and
economic systems and the environment, than are other groups of
scientists with an interest in environmental problems. Some
ecologists seem to recognize these facts (see Sklar and Costanza,
1991). For this reason alone, geographers should be making
an indispensable contribution to the development of spatial
modelling of the interaction of humans with environmental
systems. With very few exceptions, they are not doing so.

It would be salutary if all geographical practitioners, and
in particular the young members of the profession, were to
heed David R. Stoddart's (1987) valiant clarion call rallying

geographers to take action on the big issues of the time. The modelling of global and regional environmental problems is surely one of the biggest contemporary issues. There may be a case for studying the spatial distribution of fish-and-chip shops in Weston-super-Mare, but there is an even more urgent case (and, rightly or wrongly, there are more funds available) for tackling the environmental consequences of global warming: if the worst-case scenarios of sea-level rise be correct, then by the end of the next century fish-and-chip shops in some coastal towns will be teeming with live fish!

Given that today modelling is so valuable a tool of research, it should surely be part of a general geographical education at undergraduate level. To this end, the least teachers of geography can do is to instruct students in simple modelling techniques. This book has tried to lay down a basis for modelling courses by providing, without becoming bogged down in mathematical arguments and notation, an outline of the processes by which models are built, and the achievements of modelling in fields related to geography. The hope is that students will be spurred into delving more deeply into mathematical modelling, and that a few may even take up the gauntlet and further their studies of modelling in the postgraduate arena.

Appendix:
Units of Measurement

Modelling environmental systems involves measuring physical quantities such as length, time, mass, area, volume, density, temperature. Most physical quantities can be expressed in terms of four selected quantities— mass (M), length (L), time (T), and temperature (θ). There are several systems of arbitrarily chosen standard units in which the magnitude of these quantities may be expressed. The *Système Internationale d'Unités* (SI) is used in this book.

Base Units

The base units, and their abbreviations, in the SI system are:

Quantity	Unit	Symbol
length	metre	m
mass	kilogram	kg
time	second	s
temperature	kelvin	K
electric current	ampere	A
luminosity	candela	cd
amount of substance	mole	mol

Kilogram and metre may also be spelt kilogramme and meter.

Derived Units

Several units can be derived from the base units. Examples include area, volume, density, velocity, acceleration, force, pressure, heat energy, and heat flux.

Force. The SI derived unit is the newton, N, defined as the force necessary to impart an acceleration of 1 metre per second per second ($1\,m/s^2$) to a mass of 1 kg.

Pressure and Stress. The SI derived unit of pressure and stress is the pascal, Pa, defined as the pressure exerted by a force of 1 N evenly

TABLE A.1. *Metric multiples and submultiples*

Prefix	Symbol	Scientific notation	Decimal notation	Description
exa	E	10^{18}	1 000 000 000 000 000 000	—
peta	P	10^{15}	1 000 000 000 000 000	—
tera	T	10^{12}	1 000 000 000 000	trillion
giga	G	10^{9}	1 000 000 000	billion
mega	M	10^{6}	1 000 000	million
myria	my	10^{4}	10 000	ten thousand
kilo	k	10^{3}	1 000	thousand
hecto	h	10^{2}	100	hundred
deca (deka)	da	10^{1}	10	ten
deci	d	10^{-1}	0.1	tenth
centi	c	10^{-2}	0.01	hundredth
milli	m	10^{-3}	0.001	thousandth
micro	μ	10^{-6}	0.000 001	millionth
nano	n	10^{-9}	0.000 000 001	billionth
pico	p	10^{-12}	0.000 000 000 001	trillionth
femto	f	10^{-15}	0.000 000 000 000 001	—
atto	a	10^{-18}	0.000 000 000 000 000 001	—

Note: The terms billion and trillion (and billionth and trillionth) here follow the US definitions, which have become widely accepted. In the UK, a milliard is a thousand million (10^{9}), and a billion is a million (10^{12}). Similarly, in the UK, the terms milliardth and billionth denote a thousand millionth and a million millionth respectively.

distributed over $1\,m^2$. Atmospheric pressures are conventionally expressed in bars or millibars ($1\,bar = 10^{5}\,Pa = 10^{5}\,N\,m$).

Work and Energy. The derived SI unit for all forms of energy is the joule, J, and is defined as the energy needed to displace a force of $1\,N$ through a distance of $1\,m$. The joule is sometimes called the newton-metre, $N\,m$. The calorie, cal, is still widely used in biology and ecology ($1\,cal \simeq 4.18\,J$; $1000\,cal = 1\,kcal = 1\,Cal$).

Power. The derived SI unit is the watt, W, defined as the power required to equal the rate of working of $1\,J/s$.

Multiples and Submultiples

A large number of multiples and submultiples are used with metric units (Table A.1). The SI system recommends that only multiples and sub-multiples of a thousand are used (10^{3}, 10^{-3}, 10^{6}, 10^{-6}, 10^{9}, 10^{-9}, etc.), and discourages the use of the prefixes hecto, deca, deci, centi, and myria. However, these 'banned' prefixes can be useful at times and are used.

Units Commonly Used in Geography and Ecology

Length. The basic unit of length in the SI system is the metre. In geography, the kilometre is the commonest multiple. A variety of submultiples is used. Note that the micrometre, µm, is often called a micron.

Area. Area has the dimensions of length squared (L^2). The basic unit of area in the SI system is the square metre, m^2. Commonly used multiples and submultiples are the square kilometre, km^2, and the square centimetre, cm^2. In land measurement the are, a, and hectare, ha, are frequently adopted as units $(1\,a = 100\,m^2; 1\,ha = 10\,000\,m^2)$.

Volume. Volume has the dimensions of length cubed (L^3). The basic unit of volume in the SI system is the cubic metre, m^3. Commonly used multiples and submultiples are the cubic kilometre, km^3, and the cubic centimetre, cm^3 (sometimes written cc). Fluid volumes are commonly expressed as litres, l, or millilitres, ml $(1\,l = 1\,dm^3; 1\,ml = 1\,cm^3)$.

Mass. Mass is the quantity of matter that a given object contains. The basic SI unit of mass is the gram (sometimes spelt gramme). In geography and the environmental sciences, commonly used submultiples for small quantities of mass are the milligram, mg, and the microgram, µg. Intermediate masses are commonly expressed in kilograms, kg, or tonnes, t $(1\,t = 1000\,kg = 1\,Mg)$. For the enormous stores of materials in the biosphere, high multiples are helpful, including megatonnes, Mt, teragrams, Tg, and gigagrams, Gg. For clarity, it is worth denoting the type of mass being referred to. So, when describing the amount of carbon in a store, we could write g C as a shorthand for grammes of carbon, and Gt C for gigatonnes of carbon.

It is hard to visualize vast quantities of materials stored in environmental systems. To put some of the figures mentioned in text in perspective, it might help to think of blocks of ice. A cubic metre of ice has a mass of $1\,t$ (assuming that the density of ice is $1\,g/cm^3$). A block of ice 100 m long, 100 m wide, and standing 100 m high would weigh $10^{12}\,g = 1\,000\,000\,t = 1000\,Gg = 1\,Tg$. A cubic kilometre of ice would weight $10^{15}\,g = 1\,000\,000\,000\,t = 1\,000\,000\,Gg = 1000\,Tg = 1\,Pg$.

Density. This is mass per unit volume, unit area, or unit length; for example, kg/m^3.

Concentration. This is the amount of a given substance in a unit amount of another substance. For material in solution, it may be expressed as the number of moles of solute in a litre of solvent. Solute concentrations may be expressed as grams per litre, g/l. Where concentrations are very small, it is common to use one of the following expressions: parts per thousand (ppt), parts per million (ppm), and parts per billion (ppb). Parts per million means the weight of a solute in a million parts of solution. To convert g/l to ppm, multiply by 1000. For example, 0.88 g/l = 880 ppm. If the concentration is measured on a volumetric basis, as is commonly the case with atmospheric constituents, then we should denote this fact by writing the concentration as parts per million by volume (ppmv). In geochemistry, concentrations are commonly expressed as milligrams per kilogram (mg/kg).

To denote concentrations of chemical species, the letter p (from the German potenz, meaning power) may be used. Everybody is probably familiar with the expression pH, meaning the concentration of hydrogen ions. The letter p may be used to denote the concentration of any substance. For instance, pCO_2 stands for the concentration of carbon dioxide.

Mass Flow. This is defined as either mass per unit time or volume per unit time. River discharge, for instance, is commonly measured as cubic metres per second (m^3/s), also styled cumecs, while the flow of suspended sediment in a river is measured as tonnes per year (t/yr). It is sometimes necessary to measure the density (intensity) of mass flow. This is the mass flow rate per unit area, and would be expressed in such units as $kg/m^2/s$.

Energy Flow. This is defined analogously to mass flow. For instance, heat flow rate may be expressed as J/s (= W). The density of the heat flow rate would be expressed as $J/m^2/s$ (= W/m^2). In meteorology, the langley, ly, was once widely used (1 ly = $cal/cm^2 \simeq 4.18 J/cm^2$).

NB. The use of more than one solidus (/) in an expression is nowadays generally frowned upon. However, in most systems of interest to geographers and environmental scientists, density of mass (and energy) flow has been traditionally expressed in a form such as kg/ha/yr. This kind of expression is unambiguous enough and is used in this book. Pedantic scientists would probably have preferred to see the less elegant alternatives—kg/(ha yr) or $kg\,ha^{-1}\,yr^{-1}$.

References

Alcamo, J., Amann, M., Hettelingh, J.-P., Holmberg, M., Hordijk, L., Kämäri, J., Kauppi, L., Kauppi, P., Kornai, G., and Mäkelä, A. (1987). 'Acidification in Europe: A Simulation Model for Evaluating Control Strategies', *Ambio*, 16: 232–45.

Bakan, S., Chlond, A., Cubasch, U., Feichter, J., Graf, H., Grassl, H., Hasselmann, K., Kirchner, I., Latif, M., Roeckner, E., Sausen, R., Schlese, U., Schriever, D., Schult, I., Schumann, U., Sielmann, F., and Welke, W. (1991). 'Climate Response to Smoke from the Burning Oil Wells in Kuwait', *Nature*, 351: 367–71.

Baker, W. L. (1989). 'A Review of Models of Landscape Change', *Landscape Ecology*, 2: 111–33.

Bartell, S. M., and Brenkert, A. L. (1991). 'A Spatial-Temporal Model of Nitrogen Dynamics in a Deciduous Forest Watershed', in M. G. Turner and R. H. Gardner (eds.), *Quantitative Methods in Landscape Ecology: The Analysis and Interpretation of Landscape Heterogeneity*, 379–98. New York: Springer.

Berry, R. J. (ed.) (1992). *Environmental Dilemmas: Ethics and Decisions*. London: Chapman and Hall.

Bertalanffy, L. von (1951). *Theoretische Biologie*, 2nd edn. Berne: A. Francke.

—— (1973). *General Systems Theory: Foundations, Principles, Applications*. Harmondsworth: Penguin.

Bethke, C. M., Harrison, W. J., Upson, C., and Altaner, S. P. (1988). 'Supercomputer Analysis of Sedimentary Basins', *Science*, 239: 261–7.

Botkin, D. B. (1992). *Forest Dynamics: An Ecological Model*. New York: Oxford Univ. Press.

—— Janak, J. F., and Wallis, J. R. (1972). 'Some Ecological Consequences of a Computer Model of Forest Growth', *Journal of Ecology*, 60: 849–73.

Browning, K. A., Allam, R. J., Ballard, S. P., Barnes, R. T. H., Bennetts, D. A., Maryon, R. H., Mason, P. J., McKenna, D., Mitchell, J. F. B., Senior, C. A., Slingo, A., and Smith, F. B. (1991). 'Environmental Effects from Burning Oil Wells in Kuwait', *Nature*, 351: 363–7.

Caldwell, L. K. (1990). *Between Two Worlds: Science, the Environmental Movement and Policy Change*. Cambridge: Cambridge Univ. Press.

CHORLEY, R. J., and KENNEDY, B. A. (1971). *Physical Geography: A Systems Approach*. London: Prentice-Hall.

COSTANZA, R., SKLAR, F. H., and WHITE, M. L. (1990). 'Modeling Coastal Landscape Dynamics', *BioScience*, 40: 91–107.

COVEY, C., THOMPSON, S. L., and SCHNEIDER, S. H. (1985). ' "Nuclear Winter": A Diagnosis of Atmospheric General Circulation Model Simulations', *Journal of Geophysical Research*, 90: 5615–28.

CROWLEY, T. J. (1991). 'Utilization of Paleoclimate Results to Validate Projections of Future Greenhouse Warming', in M. E. Schlesinger (ed.), *Greenhouse-Gas-Induced Climatic Change: A Critical Appraisal of Simulations and Observations*, 35–45. Amsterdam: Elsevier.

CRUTZEN, P. J., and BIRKS, J. W. (1982). 'The Atmosphere After a Nuclear War: Twilight at Noon', *Ambio*, 11: 114–25.

EHRLICH, P. R., SAGAN, C., KENNEDY, D., and ROBERTS, W. O. (1984). *The Cold and the Dark: The World After Nuclear War*. London: Sidgwick and Jackson.

EMANUEL, W. R., SHUGART, H. H., and STEVENSON, M. P. (1985). 'Climatic Change and the Broad-Scale Distribution of Terrestrial Ecosystem Complexes', *Climatic Change*, 7: 29–43.

ESSER, G. (1987). 'Sensitivity of Global Carbon Pools and Fluxes to Human and Potential Climatic Impacts', *Tellus*, 39B: 245–60.

—— (1989). 'Global Land-Use Changes from 1860 to 1980 and Future Projections to 2500', *Ecological Modelling*, 44: 307–16.

—— (1991). 'Osnabrück Biosphere Model: Structure, Construction, Results', in G. Esser and D. Overdieck (eds.), *Modern Ecology: Basic and Applied Aspects*, 679–709. Amsterdam: Elsevier.

—— and KOHLMAIER, G. H. (1991). 'Modelling Terrestrial Sources of Nitrogen, Phosphorus, Sulphur and Organic Carbon to Rivers', in E. T. Degens, S. Kempe, and J. E. Richey (eds.), *Biogeochemistry of Major World Rivers*, 297–322. Chichester: Wiley.

—— and LIETH, H. (1989). 'Decomposition in Tropical Rain Forests Compared with Other Parts of the World', in H. Lieth and M. J. A. Werger (eds.), *Tropical Rain Forest Ecosystems*, 571–80. Amsterdam: Elsevier.

FORRESTER, J. W. (1971). *World Dynamics*. Cambridge, Mass.: Wright-Allen.

GOUDIE, A. (1990). *The Human Impact on the Natural Environment*, 3rd edn. Oxford: Blackwell.

GOUDRIAAN, J., and KETNER, P. (1984). 'A Simulation Study for the Global Carbon Cycle, Including Man's Impact on the Biosphere', *Climatic Change*, 6: 167–92.

HANSEN, J., RIND, D., DELGENIO, A., LACIS, A., LEBEDEFF, S., PRATHER, M., and RUEDY, R. (1991). 'Regional Greenhouse Climate Effects', in M. E. Schlesinger (ed.), *Greenhouse-Gas-Induced Climatic Change: A*

Critical Appraisal of Simulations and Observations, 211–29. Amsterdam: Elsevier.

HARWELL, M. A., and HUTCHINSON, T. C. (1985). *Environmental Consequences of Nuclear War*, iii: *Ecological and Agricultural Effects*. Chichester: Wiley.

HENDERSON-SELLERS, A., and McGUFFIE, K. (1987). *A Climate Modelling Primer*. Chichester: Wiley.

HOFFERT, M. I. (1991). 'The Effects of Solar Variability on Climate', in M. E. Schlesinger (ed.), *Greenhouse-Gas-Induced Climatic Change: A Critical Appraisal of Simulations and Observations*, 413–28. Amsterdam: Elsevier.

HOUGHTON, J. T., CALLANDER, B. A., and VARNEY, S. K. (eds.) (1992). *Climatic Change 1992: The Supplementary Report to the IPCC Scientific Assessment*. Cambridge: Cambridge Univ. Press.

—— JENKINS, G. J., and EPHRAUMS, J. J. (eds.) (1990). *Climate Change: The IPCC Assessment*. Cambridge: Cambridge Univ. Press.

HUGGETT, R. J. (1980). *Systems Analysis in Geography*. Oxford: Clarendon Press.

—— (1985). *Earth Surface Systems*. Heidelberg: Springer.

—— (1991). *Climate, Earth Processes and Earth History*. Heidelberg: Springer.

JENNY, H. (1941). *Factors of Soil Formation: A System of Quantitative Pedology*. New York: McGraw-Hill.

KESSELL, S. R. (1975). 'The Glacier National Park Basic Resources and Fire Ecology Model', *Bulletin of the Ecological Society of America*, 56: 49.

KOESTLER, A. (1967). *The Ghost in the Machine*. London: Hutchinson.

—— (1978). *Janus: A Summing Up*. London: Hutchinson.

LEAN, J., and WARRILOW, D. A. (1989). 'Simulation of the Regional Climatic Impact of Amazon Deforestation', *Nature*, 342: 411–13.

MacCRACKEN, M. C., CUBASCH, U., GATES, W. L., HARVEY, L. D. D., HUNT, B. G., KATZ, R., LORENZ, E. N., MANABE, S., McAVANEY, B., McFARLAND, N., MEEHL, G. A., MELESHKO, V. P., ROBOCK, A., STENCHIKOV, G. L., STOUFFER, R. J., WANG, W.-C., WASHINGTON, W. M., WATTS, R. G., and ZEBIAK, S. E. (1991). 'Working Group 2: A Critical Appraisal of Model Simulations', in M. E. Schlesinger (ed.), *Greenhouse-Gas-Induced Climatic Change: A Critical Appraisal of Simulations and Observations*, 583–91. Amsterdam: Elsevier.

MANNION, A. M. (1991). *Global Environmental Change: A Natural and Cultural Environmental History*. Harlow: Longman.

MATTHEWS, E. (1983). 'Global Vegetation and Land Use: New High-Resolution Data Bases for Climate Studies', *Journal of Climate and Applied Meteorology*, 22: 474–87.

MAY, R. M. (1973). *Stability and Complexity in Model Ecosystems*.

Princeton, NJ: Princeton Univ. Press.

MINTZER, I. (ed.) (1992). *The Challenge of Responsible Development in a Warming World*. Cambridge: Cambridge Univ. Press.

MOORE, I. D., GRAYSON, R. B., and LADSON, A. R. (1991). 'Digital Terrain Modelling: A Review of Hydrological, Geomorphological, and Biological Applications', *Hydrological Processes*, 5: 3–30.

MORGAN, M. A. (1967). 'Hardware Models in Geography', in R. J. Chorley and P. Haggett (eds.), *Models in Geography*, 727–74. London: Methuen.

ODUM, H. T. (1971). *Environment, Power, and Society*. New York: Wiley.

—— (1983). *Systems Ecology: An Introduction*. New York: Wiley.

O'RIORDAN, T. (1988). 'Future Directions for Environmental Policy', in D. C. Pitt (ed.), *The Future of the Environment: The Social Dimensions of Conservation and Ecological Alternatives*, 168–98. London: Routledge.

OVERPECK, J. T., RIND, D., and GOLDBERG, R. (1990). 'Climate-Induced Changes in Forest Disturbance and Vegetation', *Nature*, 343: 51–3.

PASTOR, J. R., and POST, W. M. (1988). 'Response of Northern Forests to CO_2-Induced Climate Change', *Nature*, 334: 55–8.

PATTEN, B. C. (1978). 'Systems Approach to the Concept of Environment', *Ohio Journal of Science*, 78: 206–22.

—— (1982). 'Environs: Relativistic Elementary Particles for Ecology', *American Scientist*, 119: 179–219.

—— (1985). 'Energy Cycling in the Ecosystem', *Ecological Modelling*, 28: 1–71.

PEARLSTINE, L., McKELLAR, H., and KITCHENS, W. (1985). 'Modelling the Impacts of a River Diversion on Bottomland Forest Communities in the Santee River Floodplain, South Carolina', *Ecological Modelling*, 29: 283–302.

PHILLIPS, J. D. (1991). 'The Human Role in Earth Surface Systems: Some Theoretical Considerations', *Geographical Analysis*, 23: 316–31.

PITTOCK, A. B., ACKERMAN, T. P., CRUTZEN, P. J., MACCRACKEN, M. C., SHAPIRO, C. S., and TURCO, R. P. (1986). *Environmental Consequences of Nuclear War*, i: *Physical and Atmospheric Effects*. Chichester: Wiley.

PROBST, J. L., and TARDY, Y. (1987). 'Long Range Streamflow and World Continental Runoff Fluctuations Since the Beginning of This Century', *Journal of Hydrology*, 94: 289–311.

PUCCIA, C. J., and LEVINS, R. (1985). *Qualitative Modeling of Complex Systems*. Cambridge, Mass.: Harvard Univ. Press.

ROHDENBURG, H. (1989). 'Methods for the Analysis of Agro-Ecosystems in Central Europe, with Emphasis on Geoecological Aspects', *Catena*, 16: 1–57.

ROTMANS, J. (1990). *IMAGE: An Integrated Model to Assess the Greenhouse Effect*. Dordrecht: Kluwer Academic.

SCHLESINGER, W. H. (1991). *Biogeochemistry: An Analysis of Global Change*. San Diego, Calif.: Academic.

SCHNEIDER, S. H. (1988). 'What Ever Happened to Nuclear Winter?', *Climatic Change*, 12: 215–20.

—— and THOMPSON, S. L. (1988). 'Simulating the Climatic Effects of Nuclear War', *Nature*, 333: 221–7.

SCHUMM, S. A. (1956). 'The Evolution of Drainage Basin Systems and Slopes in Badlands at Perth Amboy, New Jersey', *Bulletin of the Geological Society of America*, 67: 597–646.

SHUGART, H. H., Jr., and WEST, D. C. (1977). 'Development of an Appalachian Deciduous Forest Succession Model and its Application to Assessment of the Impact of the Chestnut Blight', *Journal of Environmental Management*, 5: 161–79.

SIMMONS, I. G. (1989). *Changing the Face of the Earth: Culture, Environment, History*. Oxford: Blackwell.

SKLAR, F. H., and COSTANZA, R. (1986). 'A Spatial Simulation of Ecosystem Succession in a Louisiana Coastal Landscape', in R. Crosbie and P. Luker (eds.), *Proceedings of the 1986 Summer Computer Simulation Conference*, 467–72. San Diego, Calif.: Society of Computer Simulation.

—— and COSTANZA, R. (1991). 'The Development of Dynamic Spatial Models for Landscape Ecology: A Review and Prognosis', in M. G. Turner and R. H. Gardner (eds.), *Quantitative Methods in Landscape Ecology: An Analysis and Interpretation of Landscape Heterogeneity*, 239–88. New York: Springer.

—— and DAY, J. W. Jr. (1990). 'Model Conceptualization', in B. C. Patten *et al.* (eds.), *Wetlands and Shallow Continental Water Bodies*, i: 625–58. The Hague: SPB Academic.

SOLOMON, A. M. (1986). 'Transient Response of Forests to CO_2-Induced Climatic Change: Simulation Modeling Experiments in Eastern North America', *Oecologia*, 68: 567–79.

STODDART, D. R. (1987). 'To Claim the High Ground: Geography for the End of the Century', *Transactions of the Institute of British Geographers*, n.s. 12: 327–36.

STRAHLER, A. N. (1980). 'Systems Theory in Physical Geography', *Physical Geography*, 1: 1–27.

—— and STRAHLER, A. H. (1973). *Environmental Geoscience*. Santa Barbara, Calif.: Hamilton.

—— —— (1974). *Introduction to Environmental Science*. Santa Barbara, Calif.: Hamilton.

THOMAS, R. W., and HUGGETT, R. J. (1980). *Modelling in Geography: A Mathematical Approach*. London: Harper and Row.

THORNTHWAITE, C. W., and MATHER, J. R. (1957). 'Instructions and Tables for Computing Potential Evapotranspiration and the Water Balance', *Publications in Climatology*, 10: 181–311.

TURCO, R. P., TOON, O. B., ACKERMAN, T. P., POLLOCK, J. B., and SAGAN, C. (1983). 'Nuclear Winter: Global Consequences of Multiple Nuclear Explosions', *Science*, 222: 1283–92.

TURNER, M. G. (1989). 'Landscape Ecology: The Effect of Pattern on Process', *Annual Review of Ecology and Systematics*, 20: 171–97.

TURNER, B. L. II, CLARK, W. C., KATES, R. W., RICHARDS, J. F., MATHEWS, J. T., MEYER, W. B. (eds.) (1990). *The Earth as Transformed by Human Action: Global and Regional Changes in the Biosphere over the Past 300 Years*. Cambridge: Cambridge Univ. Press with Clark University.

VÖRÖSMARTY, C. J., and MOORE, B. III (1991). 'Modeling Basin-Scale Hydrology in Support of Physical Climate and Biogeochemical Studies: An Example Using the Zambezi River', in E. F. Wood (ed.), *Land Surface–Atmospheric Interactions: Parameterization and Analysis for Climate Modeling*, 271–311. Dordrecht: Kluwer Academic.

—— —— GRACE, A. L., GILDEA, M. P., MELILLO, J. M., PETERSON, B. J., RASTETTER, E. B., and STEUDLER, P. A. (1989). 'Continental Scale Models of Water Balance and Fluvial Transport: An Application to South America', *Global Biogeochemical Cycles*, 3: 241–65.

WASHINGTON, W. M., and MEEHL, G. A. (1991). 'Characteristics of Coupled Atmosphere–Ocean CO_2 Sensitivity Experiments with Different Ocean Formulations', in M. E. Schlesinger (ed.), *Greenhouse-Gas-Induced Climatic Change: A Critical Appraisal of Simulations and Observations*, 79–110. Amsterdam: Elsevier.

WEBB, D. J. (1991). 'FRAM: the Fine Resolution Antarctic Model', in D. G. Farmer and M. J. Rycroft (eds.), *Computer Modelling in the Environmental Sciences*, 1–14. Oxford: Clarendon Press.

WIGLEY, T. M. L. (1989). 'Possible Climate Change Due to SO_2-Derived Cloud Condensation Nuclei', *Nature*, 339: 365–7.

—— (1992). 'Implications for Climate and Sea Level of Revised IPCC Emission Scenarios', *Nature*, 357: 293–300.

Index

open system 21, 25
open system theory 21
optical depth 91, 93, 94, 96
ordinary difference equation 27, 29
ordinary differential equation 27, 29
Osnabrück biosphere model 118, 180
output function 40, 41, 42, 43

parameterization 82, 137
partial difference equation 27, 29
partial differential equation 27, 28
partitioning 52, 59, 138
pasture 115, 137, 138
PC (Personal Computer) 48, 180
Perth Amboy, New Jersey 5
phosphorus 104
phytomass 118, 121, 122, 125, 127
phytomass share factor 122
pixel 6, 32, 181
plantation 115
population storage equation 39
precipitation 10, 12, 13, 73, 83, 94, 96, 97, 98, 114, 119, 122, 123, 128, 129, 137, 144, 155, 164
principle of energy conservation 38, 39
probabilistic model 21
process laws 38

radiative-convective model (RCM) 80, 91, 107
rainfall 67, 83, 130, 131, 132, 136, 137, 138, 164, 166, 169
raster 31
rate constant 40, 44, 56, 58, 122
reforestation 107, 115, 118, 122, 127
Regional Acidification Information
and Simulation (RAINS) model 139
relief model 4
remotely sensed image 6, 177, 181
renewable energy sources 107, 118
residence time 44, 95, 103
respiration 37, 38, 40, 43, 52, 54, 58
river discharge 128, 135, 158, 169
river flow 127, 136, 172
root sloughage 37
rounding error 46
rules of flow 39, 42
rules of storage 37
Runge–Kutta method 50, 105
runoff 10, 127, 128, 129, 132, 133, 134, 135, 138, 144

salinity 167, 168, 169, 170, 171
Santee River, South Carolina 157
scale model 4, 5
scaling 5
sea-level-rise model 105, 110, 111
semi-desert 115
semi-Markov model 29
Schefferville, Quebec 150, 153
signed digraph 8, 10, 13
slope gradient 13
snowfall 130, 131, 132
snowmelt 129, 130, 132, 133, 144
snowpack 132, 133, 144
soil acidification 140, 142, 144
soil carbon pool 118
soil moisture 82, 128, 129, 130, 131, 132, 135, 138
soil moisture retention curve 131
soil water storage 13, 131
soot 102
South America 128, 129, 135, 138
spatial domain 30, 31, 32, 38, 65, 73, 129, 180, 181
spatial gradient 65